SPIRIT-LED

WHEN YOU FOLLOW GOD'S LEADING

TRICIA DEBOER

Spirit-Led: When You Follow God's Leading

Trilogy Christian Publishers
A Wholly Owned Subsidary of Trinity Broadcasting Network
2442 Michelle Drive, Tustin, CA 92780

For information about special discounts for bulk purchases, please contact Trilogy Christian Publishing. Rights Department, 2442 Michelle Drive, Tustin, CA 92780.

Trilogy Christian Publishing/TBN and colophon are trademarks of Trinity Broadcasting Network.

Trilogy Disclaimer: The views and content expressed in this book are those of the author and may not necessarily reflect the views and doctrine of Trilogy Christian Publishing or the Trinity Broadcasting Network.

COVER PHOTOGRAPHY BY: Mariah Mathews with Whimsy Photography
PHOTOGRAPHY: Mariah Mathews with Whimsy Photography
LOCATION: Pretty Place, Cleveland, SC

AUTHOR CONTACT: Tricia DeBoer, www.twiggygrace.com, twiggy728@gmail.com

Manufactured in the United States of America
10 9 8 7 6 5 4 3 2 1

Library of Congress Cataloging-in-Publication Data is available.

ISBN: 978-1-63769-110-6
E-ISBN: 978-1-63769-111-3

DEDICATION

Before anyone, I want to thank my Lord and Savior for putting the desire to write this book in my heart in the first place. He asked me to share things I was never planning on sharing because He knew someone needed to read it.

I also want to thank my favorite boys: my sweet, patient, and loving husband, and my adorable, precious son Isaiah, for loving me through this journey. Isaiah, may you live out your God-given destiny at a young age, and may you be a Kingdom warrior!

Thanks to Andrea Patterson Jasmin, for your dedication and encouragement as my first editor to help make my book dream a reality.

Thank you, also, to my prayer warriors. Without you praying for me when I needed it this book would still be unfinished. I love you all.

CONTENTS

Introduction 7

Chapter 1: In the Park 11
Chapter 2: He's the One 23
Chapter 3: Nuggets of Wisdom 31
Chapter 4: Three Fuzzy Pillows 45
Chapter 5: The Blonde Lady at the Door 53
Chapter 6: You Will Have a Son 63
Chapter 7: Heaven Sent Empanadas 71
Chapter 8: December 5th 81
Chapter 9: This Mama Needs a Baby 91
Chapter 10: My Vision 101

INTRODUCTION

This book idea was placed in my heart about seven months ago. I wasn't planning on sharing some of these stories, but God has a funny way of making you do what you don't want to do. As I was writing each chapter in the early mornings when the Lord would wake me up, the names of future chapters would come to me. As He woke me up at 4:00 a.m., 5:00 a.m., or 6:00 a.m., I would put my timer on my phone for an hour and my fingers would just type away. I was amazed at how the words were just coming to me. Before I knew it, I had written a chapter. He really wanted me to finish this book. I could feel Him nudging me many days. The prayer warriors He surrounded me with were no joke! He sent me such amazing women who were a step ahead of me. I know He sent them to show me that if they could write a book, so could I. Meeting so many women who were in the process of writing a book really helped me when I was thinking about writing a book.

I'm going to be very transparent. I'm a private person. I'm friendly, but I'm not one to share about my private life. So, when I heard God say, "These crazy experiences that you went through are not just for you to keep to yourself. You are going to share it with the world," you can just imagine my response. *Absolutely not, Lord! Absolutely not!*

I'd like to share something with you that happened to me which will help you understand why I was so apprehensive. For as long as I can remember, I have always worked in a church youth group. I was president of my youth group because my uncle was a pastor. In college, I was a leader with "Young Life" (a youth organization), and when I came back from college, I was a youth group leader in my church. So, I've been helping out with different church youth groups for more than 20 years. I preface all of this to tell you what happened to me at a church that will remain nameless.

I was leading a group of girls that I just adored, and it was going so great that year. Out of nowhere, a lady whose position oversaw the girl leaders made the decision of telling me that I was no longer going to be the leader of the group of girls I had been leading for about a year. She said she wanted me to lead a few girls on the praise team instead. I told her I would pray about it, and to my surprise, she said it wasn't an option. I was so hurt. I cried a lot, and none of it made sense at all to me. I ended up leading the girls on the praise team and met some really sweet teen girls that still have a hold on my heart. In the end, God always has His reasons.

Without going into much detail, I found out months later why I was moved from the group of girls that I just loved so much. One of the girls was seeing a demon and it was taunting her. Since I had had similar experiences, I let her know she was not crazy, and I shared with her that she had to rebuke the demon and tell it to leave. So, because I told this teenager what to do and did not give her scripture, I was removed from the girl group that I was leading.

After that experience, I was definitely never open to sharing my experiences again. That closed me from sharing. But God has a funny way of, again, making you do things you don't want to do. I left the church a few months later because I was so hurt. The Lord led me to another amazing group of girls, and I also met more people who had had similar experiences like me. God has perfect timing. Don't ever doubt that.

His timing is everything. I had to go through some more experiences ten years later that I will share more about in the following chapters. God led me to this other church to meet some more amazing girls that God was going to use me for in their lives. This church encouraged me to be more courageous and open with my faith. A conference that I went to in March of this year catapulted me to my destiny, which was writing this book and sharing my heart.

If you are wondering what your calling, purpose, or destiny is, then this is the book for you! We all have a calling, but it's up to us to make it come alive. Are you ready? Come along with me on this crazy journey of my life. We all have a God-given destiny!

CHAPTER 1

In the Park

You dear children, are from God and have
overcome them, because the one who is in you
is greater than the one who is in the world.

1 JOHN 4:4

My life has always been full of crazy experiences and adventures. When my husband would give me a birthday or anniversary card he always added, "I love you and all your crazy ideas and adventures." One of my most memorable travels was to Croatia. My step-father is from Croatia, and for my seventeenth birthday he wanted me to meet his mom. He took my mom and me to Croatia for an entire month. That was such an amazing experience! I was able to visit Italy while I was there, which was my lifelong dream!

I was starting my senior year of high school upon coming back from my trip and I thought to myself, *How am I going to top that trip for my senior summer?* I was looking for something fun and exciting to do before I started my college life. A friend of mine told me about a traveling choir that traveled to all types of cities and countries around the world. That definitely piqued my interest! I started to look into it right away and soon found out it was going to be really expensive. *How on earth would I be able to come up with all that money?* When God has something in mind for you He makes a way.

This new journey was not only going to be a start to a new adventure, but it would also teach me how incredible of a God He is. I was running out of ideas when I decided to share my concern with my high school choir director. He was such a wonderful listening ear during my high school years. He had a very tough exterior, but he was a huge teddy bear on the inside, and he always believed in me when I couldn't believe in myself. When the auditions for the school musical started, he encouraged me to try out even though I didn't think I had a chance of making it. I ended up getting a part in the play and enjoyed every minute of it! He also excitedly pushed me to try out for a state choir that he thought I would really enjoy. The week I was trying out I ended up getting a cold. I thought to myself, *Now how am I going to make tryouts for the soprano part when I sound like a fog horn?* The day of my audition my sweet choir director bought me some hot tea with lemon and recommended I try out for the alto part instead of the soprano part and I actually made the choir! Without him believing in me I would have never been able to enjoy these two incredible opportunities that I have some amazing memories of!

One day after I shared my desire to try out for the traveling choir, he asked me to come to his office because he wanted to talk to me about something. I had no idea what he wanted to talk about. I walked into his office and sat down and asked him what he wanted to talk about. He then proceeded to hand me an envelope. When I opened it, to my complete surprise, it contained a scholarship from my school in the exact amount I needed in order to be a part of the traveling choir! Won't God do it! When He wants you to do something, He will make a way!

God knew that I had to go on this new adventure to show me more of His incredible love and provision and to grow me to be more like Him. The experience was like no other.

We traveled on a bus covering 12 states along the Eastern Coast, and at each destination we had to perform one to two concerts a day. It was exhausting and exhilarating all at the same time. When we got to our designated city, we would have dinner waiting for us, then we were assigned to our host family for the night. Meeting so many different families and seeing so many different homes were probably some of my favorite parts of the entire experience! In Pennsylvania, I got to stay with the sweetest elderly couple on a beautiful farm. We had fresh cow's milk and amazing fresh muffins for breakfast. They were delicious! Another time I got to stay with a single lady in Canada in her penthouse on the 17th floor, which had an incredible view.

One of our concerts, I believe it was in Virginia, had one of the biggest impacts on me. It was at a veteran's home. We were having a picnic outside when all of a sudden, we saw a man in uniform marching in the woods. We asked our guide about it, and he said that this certain gentleman thinks he is still in the army and marches every morning in his uniform for miles. This was the first of many heartbreaking moments we would see. A few hours later we performed on this outside stage for the veterans.

It was a beautiful time, seeing these elderly men who had been through so much with smiles on their faces. After the concert, we were always encouraged to meet and mingle.

I approached an older gentleman who looked blind and who was being guided by a couple of other gentlemen. They were so kind and loving and thanked us for singing for them. I let them know that it was our pleasure to be there and to get to know them all. Later I found out that the older gentleman I thought was blind wasn't really blind. He had seen so much in the war and in his time in the service that his brain turned off his sight. So many of these men were so hurt because of what they had seen or been through that it made them disabled, and they had to live at this center to be taken care of. My heart ached for these men. I was blessed to have met them. I was thankful that we put a smile on their faces that day.

It was at places like these that the Lord allowed His light to shine through us and be beacons of light to the hurting. We were His hands and feet. These were special times, where we took full advantage of sharing the gospel with the lost. It was a beautiful time to hear their stories and to also remind them that Jesus loves them, died for them, and is still crazy about them.

During our travels, we were on the bus a lot. We were encouraged to listen to only Christian music and at this time we all had what was called a "Walkman," which was the way we listened to music at the time. (You may have to google "Walkman.") I was from New Jersey, and I had never even heard of any Christian singers. I was soon introduced to some Christian artists like Sandi Patti, Jeremy Camp, and Michael W. Smith to name a few.

Back then the only way to listen to music was via tape. (You may want to google that too, for some more laughs.) Right now, we listen to music through applications on our phones like iTunes, Pandora or Spotify. (There is no telling how we will listen to music in the future.) There were no cell phones at that time, so we played a lot of card games like Yuker and Spades. It was such a fun time. We got to know each other really well, and amazingly enough, we didn't even miss not having cell phones.

There was a week during my trip that I kept thinking about my friend back home. I missed her and she was on my mind a lot. We were really close, and we hung out together a lot. Since we didn't have cell phones then, all I could do was pray that she was okay and talk to her when I could use my host family's phone.

That weekend was my birthday, and I was sad that we wouldn't be together to celebrate. Our choir was headed to Ocala, Florida, and we were going to have a concert at a church that night. When we got to the church we were greeted with a delicious dinner and then we were introduced to our host family. When I met my host family, they were so nice. They told us that we were welcome to use their phones to call whomever we wanted, and that we could also stay on the phone as long as we wanted. God is so good. That is exactly what I needed—to call my family and friend from home.

We had our concert that night at a small, quaint church. Our choir director always encouraged us to speak from our hearts between songs when we felt led. We were told that if God had something He wanted us to share, then He would let us know. I had never spoken during any concert until that day. She said our hearts would start beating fast and it would not go away until we shared what God was placing on our heart at that moment. Well, that night, after a certain song, my heart started racing. I thought to myself, *Not now. Not in front of all these people!* So, I took a step forward, and my choir director handed me the microphone.

I started talking about my friend from home and how she had been on my mind all week and I felt like she needed prayer. I said that sometimes God brings people up in our minds because they need us to stand in the gap in prayer for them. That's all I can remember of what I said. Mind you this was thirty plus years ago when I was eighteen. I'm thankful I can even remember that I went on this tour.

After the concert, I had a few people that approached me and wanted to pray for my friend. Then a few more joined us, and before I knew it, we had eight people in a circle holding hands uplifting my friend in prayer. God is so amazing how He touches our hearts this way. None of these strangers knew my friend, but they felt led to pray for her. That was just beautiful! Little did I know at the time that my friend needed all the prayers she could get.

We got to the host family's house where they had some snacks for us, and once again they encouraged us to call whomever we wanted. I quickly got settled in my room and called my friend. It was so nice to hear her voice, and everything sounded normal. I thought, *Wow, maybe I was wrong and she didn't need prayer after all.* I was surely mistaken. I started to tell her about how things were going on my tour and started talking about all the amazing things that God was showing me.

This is when things started getting weird. Every time I mentioned God or Jesus she would excuse herself and said. "I'll be right back." It kept happening and I finally said, "What is going on?" She told me that anytime I mentioned the word "God," she felt like she was going to be sick.

I decided to ask her about what she had been up to lately. She started telling me about some strange things that were happening to her. I then asked her about the places she had visited. She told me that she had gone to a new church, so I asked her what it was like. She proceeded to tell me that she was learning about some new stuff. I then asked her what kind of stuff she was learning. She said how to move pennies with her mind without touching them among a few other things.

I thought to myself, *What in the world?* My friend had gone to a satanic church! I was floored, to say the least. She wanted to tell me more, and I just changed the subject. I started to pray as she kept talking about something else. I was so lost and confused and didn't know what to do. After I prayed, I started to look for scripture. I started quoting scripture with the word Jesus in it. She kept running to the bathroom and I told her, "I don't care if you get sick. I'm reading scripture to you." I then got the person who I was rooming with at the time and told her to pray and to help me find more scriptures. This went on and on for a while until I finally felt some peace. The tour was ending in a few weeks so I told her I would be praying for her and that I would see her soon. This was all very new for me. This was nothing that I expected, but now it all made sense—the eight people who prayed for her and the fact that I couldn't get her out of my mind.

I asked different people in the choir if they had experienced anything like this. I soon found out that when someone is demon possessed it was very common for them to feel like they were going to be sick when the name of Jesus or God was spoken. It all made sense. I felt such an urgency to go home to help my friend out. Everyone else was reading this book called *This Present Darkness* by Frank E. Peretti. I'm not too fond of scary movies so I kept telling everyone to "have fun with that one." Not my cup of tea. Little did I know that instead of reading the book I would be experiencing what was in the book!

After traveling for 54 days and covering 12 states I was finally home! It felt so good to sleep in my bed and be in my room, but the strangest thing happened when I got back. I could not watch TV or listen to the radio. I had been away from it all for so long that it felt foreign to me; it felt very odd. So, I would hang out in my room listening to my Christian music tapes that I had acquired on my trip. We were told by our choir director that this sort of thing would possibly happen. She told us to stay in contact with the other choir members, stay in the Word, and encourage one another. I'm so glad she had shared that because I would have thought I was crazy!

The next day I decided to call my friend and ask her to come over and hang out with me. (Before I go into what the call was like, let me give you this backstory first. One of my friends from the tour told me that there was a part in the book where a character in the book who was possessed said someone was shooting lights in their eyes. This was referring to a Christian who was talking to him and that he felt God's light shooting towards them. So back to the conversation with my friend.) It all started out normal. She was excited to come over and was headed out the door to see me soon. Before the conversation ended my friend said these exact words, "I'm excited to see you, but I'm afraid you are going to shoot lights in my eyes." I almost dropped the phone! *Is this really happening?* I asked myself. *Why was I experiencing things from this book?* I still didn't want to read it so my friend summarized it for me so that I got the gist. I was still scared to read the book.

My friend came over and it was so good to see her. I had missed her so much! Fifty-four days is a long time to be away from home. I showed her the Bible that our choir director gave all of us, which I still have, and she loved it. It was a teen Bible with some great questions and answers that a lot of teens have. She fell in love with my Bible, so I told her we would share it. The name of the Bible is *The Transformer Bible*, in case you want to get it.

We soon decided to go to a nearby park and walk around. Not sure why we decided to go to the park when we usually would go shopping at the mall, but for whatever reason we chose the park. Once again it started off normal, with us laughing and reminiscing of our high school experiences. As we walked around we realized that they were having a display of roses. The ground went for miles with all different colored roses. It was so beautiful.

As we were walking, we passed by a bird on the ground that was in a puddle of water, and the sun was shining on it so beautifully. It looked like it was bathing in it. It was the cutest thing!

As I showed it to my friend, she said, "That's just a dumb bird rolling around in a mud puddle. What's up with you, Trish?"

I thought it was a little odd that she saw a mud puddle and I saw a clean little puddle where a cute bird was bathing, but I put it behind me and kept walking and talking.

Then I said, "These roses are so beautiful. Look at the different colors."

She said, "It's just some dumb flowers. I don't see the big deal."

Once again, I thought to myself, *Why are we seeing things so differently?* And I brushed it off and thought, *Maybe it's because of this tour. Things have been a bit odd since I've been back.* Then we just kept walking some more.

We decided to sit at a bench overlooking a pond. We sat there and talked for a bit, and I tried not to bring anything up that would cause a weird reaction. As I sat on the bench and looked around, I admired the beautiful blue sky with white puff clouds, and I noticed a mom pushing her baby in a stroller while walking around the pond. I also saw some kids swinging on swings on the left side of the pond a good distance away. I didn't bother mentioning it to my friend because I was sure that she would say something negative again.

All of a sudden, while I was in mid-sentence, out of nowhere came her voice saying, "Satan rules the earth."

Confused at what was just said I thought to myself, *Did she really just say that?* My response back was, "What did you just say?"

It then looked right at me, and said it again, "Satan rules the earth!"

At this point I realized that this was not my friend speaking, and as this thing looked at me I saw that its eyes were light and bright green. Her eyes would normally change from blue to green, but I had never seen them that light of a green before. I'm sorry, but when a person's eyes turn bright, light green and they give you a piercing glare you may get a little freaked out. And yes, I did!

I started asking myself, *Do I run? Do I yell?* At that point, I looked around and everything was black, white, and grey. I looked out and the mom pushing the stroller was nowhere in sight and neither were the kids swinging on the swings. I was in this grey world with no one in sight! If I ran this demon would probably chase me, and if I ran where would I run? And if I get to a house will there be anyone in it? I was freaking out!

All of a sudden, I had this feeling in my spirit nudging me and reminding me, *You can pray.* I know the Holy Spirit was reminding me to pray. I was so frantic that I had forgotten all about praying. So that's exactly what I started to do right away! I started to say, "Lord Jesus, please help me! Please bring my friend back and make this demon go away, and please protect me and surround me like a bubble!" It's all I could muster up.

I was sitting on the bench with my feet flat on the ground facing the water. The next thing I knew I was facing my friend, hugging my bent knees. God actually moved me from the prior position.

You may be asking why God would move me. It was for a reason. I then noticed that there were about 10 to 15 black flies swarming around her feet and all of a sudden one bit her and she yelped, "Ouch!" Then she grabbed the fly between her fingers and flicked it off. Now, my friend would never kill an ant, let alone a big fly. I believe it was her saying "ouch" and the demon squishing the fly because she did not like bugs. The next thing I knew she was now hugging her bent knees and crying.

I then realized my friend was back! Hallelujah! So, I asked her if she remembered anything and she said, "All I remember is you talking about something, and I guess I just blanked out." *Wow, so now I have to tell her everything!* So, I proceeded to tell her everything that just happened, and you guessed it, she didn't believe any of it and still doesn't. It's okay, because it was for me to experience, not her. The story isn't over though.

Right after she told me she didn't believe me, I saw the beautiful blue sky with the white puffy clouds, the mom pushing the stroller was back, along with the kids on the swings. When all was right with the world again, I noticed that she was seeing pretty things. *Yeah!* She was commenting about a squirrel that had come right up to her and how pretty it was. Then some ducks came up to her and some birds and rabbits and, before I knew it, there were a bunch of different animals surrounding her.

God was wanting to show her His beauty that she probably couldn't see or appreciate for quite a while. Isn't God amazing? He allowed me to see what she was seeing. The grey, the sadness, the world without its beauty, just so I could sympathize and understand what she had been going through and seeing. He also allowed her to see the grey world without His beauty so that He could bring her out of it and show her the grandeur of Him and His amazing creation that we so often take for granted. I will never tire of seeing a beautiful sunset, sunrise, or even being on a sandy shore with the waves splashing at my feet. When I am at a beach and when I look out to the waves I'm always reminded of God's never-ending love. Just like the waves that never stop coming to the shore, God's love never stops coming to us. We are always lavished in His love! What an amazing God we love and serve!

LET'S REFLECT

You may or may not have experienced something like this, and either way, that is okay. Can you think of a time when God may have been speaking to you—in that small still voice, like an inner knowing? Have you had a situation that you feel God had His hand on?

Take a moment to close your eyes and ask God to show you a time where He wanted to teach you something, but you never took the time to ask Him what He wanted you to learn or see from it. Take a deep breath and start writing down your experience and reflect on what God may have been trying to show you.

What have you learned through this experience?

What was the spirit trying to tell you?

CHAPTER 2

He's the One

Love is patient, love is kind. It does not boast, it is not proud. It does not dishonor others, it is not self-seeking, it is not easily angered, it keeps no record of wrongs.

1 COR. 13:4-5

A few years later after the experience at the park, little did I know that I would meet my lifelong best friend. You know when people say you will meet the right guy when you're not even looking? Yup, that's exactly how it happened to me.

I had just come back from college, and it was the summer of my junior year. My best friend from college was moving back to her home to attend a college closer to home. I was devastated, lonely, and I missed her like crazy!

I was coming back to a town that never felt like home, and I left behind such wonderful friends in college that—although I had only been there three years—had become family. Every Thursday night a bunch of us would get together and watch the show *Friends*. I think I loved the show so much because it reminded me of my group of friends. So, to say I felt lonely was an understatement. I had prayed to God before I came home that he would send me a best friend. I knew that summer was going to be so hard without one.

A friend from church had told me about a college and career group that they had started at our church. To be honest, I wasn't too excited about it because all I wanted to do was go back to college and see my "family." I still ended up going because I had nothing else to do. My first day there was a little awkward. I'm an ENFJ, which means I am very extraverted, I love to be around people, and I'm normally not shy. (I would encourage you to take this test. The test is called Meyer Briggs Personality Assessment. It will define what your personality is, who you are, and why. It was very helpful for me. I find these personality tests so fascinating.) In this case I wasn't very social. I actually felt like an awkward kid who wore two different colored socks to her first day of kindergarten.

So, I walked in and saw a couple of people that I recognized and sat with them. The group was surprisingly enjoyable. Afterwards, a few of us decided to go get some ice-cream at Friendly's. While we were there a few other people showed up and sat with us, and it ended up being a very fun night. I thought to myself, *Maybe this summer won't turn out too bad after all.*

One day our college and career group decided to go white water rafting. I was excited because these people I had ice-cream with the first day ended up being my close friends. I ended up in a raft with a couple of my guy friends, and we had a blast. That day there were no rapids. The only thing there was 100-degree weather! It was so hot that we all ended up jumping out of our raft and pushing it down the river. We ended up having a massive water fight, and I laughed till I almost peed in my pants. I ended up having a great time.

Another day I wanted to go to the beach, which was a couple hours away. I invited the whole college and career class so no one would feel left out. Out of all the people I invited only four of us

Tricia DeBoer

ended up going, including myself. It ended up being my friend from high school and two guys that always came out with us anytime we went out after group. They always made us laugh and almost pee our pants every time we hung out. I knew we were going to have a great time! We ended up going to Long Beach Island which is a beautiful beach on the Jersey shore.

We were hanging out for a while on the beach having a good time. Just so you know, I was not interested in either of these guys; they were just friends. But I found myself staring at one of the guys named Greg. He was tall, handsome, a Christian man, and super fun to be around. I don't know if it was that he looked so cute in his bathing suit and adorable du rag on his head, but something was working. Little did I know that at the same time he was having the same thing going on in his head about me. Maybe it was my polka dot bikini? All I know is that the more time we spent together the more attracted I became to this guy.

We all decided to hang out at my friend's house after we got back from the beach and ordered pizza, watched a movie, and hung out and laughed until about 2:00 a.m. I kept asking myself, *What in the world is going on with me? Where are these crazy feelings coming from?* Can I just say God has a funny way of making things happen when we least expect it?

The next day was Sunday, and we were all very tired, probably because of all the laughing, being in the sun all day, and the fact that we barely got any sleep. After church, we would always hang out outside and talked about where we wanted to go out to eat after church. That day was a little different. We were all in a circle talking when the leader of our college and career church, who happened to be Greg's brother-in-law, came over and said, "So Greg, you find anyone to go riding up to the mountains with yet?"

And he looked right at me and said, "I'm trying to. Trish do you want to ride with us?"

So of course, I said, "Yes!" I was in a dress, but I was going even if I had to stop at a store and buy something quick on the way up the mountains.

In mid thought Greg's sister said, "Don't worry, you can borrow something of mine. You look like you wear the same size as me. You can't ride a motorcycle in a dress," she said with a smile.

We went back to their place and changed, and then we headed up the mountain. What a day! We had so much fun, and the ride up there was gorgeous—and so was my driver. After our ride, we went back to his sister's house so I could get changed and ended up watching a movie and once again I stayed there until about 2:00 a.m. He walked me to my car and told me that he had a really great time and gave me a hug. I left on cloud nine with the biggest smile on my face that wouldn't go away.

That week he called my house and my mom said, "It's that cute guy from church on the phone!" I'm not going to lie, my heart skipped a beat when I heard her say that. He ended up asking me out that night and said he didn't want to tell me where he was taking me because he wanted it to be a surprise. We ended up going on our first date that weekend. I still remember it like it was yesterday. Our first date was August 4th. I also remember that as I was getting ready in my room I thought to myself, *I could marry this guy*! But then I thought to myself, *If we break up, I'm going to have to find a different church. Because that would be awkward.* Then I grabbed my purse and walked downstairs.

He was waiting for me in the living room, looking all cute in his cutoff jeans and salmon colored shirt. He was looking mighty fine! He opened the door for me, and off we went. He ended up

Tricia DeBoer

taking me to a cute little restaurant at the beach called Wharf-side. It was so pretty. We got a seat with a great view overlooking the bay—it was quite romantic. He said grace before we ate, and we both ordered the shrimp plate. Side note: I ate a lot during my college years, so when I was done, I asked if he was going to finish his shrimp. Little did I know that prior to me all his dates had only asked for a salad (not me!), so it was actually refreshing to him that I ate normal and didn't just order a salad.

After dinner, we took a walk on the beach and talked for a really long time. We shared our salvation stories and what God was doing in our lives at that time. He also shared with me about his list. You're probably wondering what kind of list. Well, he had made a list in high school about what he wanted in a wife. Would you believe I was everything on his list! He said that he wanted a Christian girl who was pretty and funny, and he said I was all of them. So of course, I had to share with him about my list that I also made in high school. I was looking for a Christian guy who was cute and musical. He said that he appreciated music, so he was everything on my list. This date was so amazing, and once again I went home on cloud nine.

God is funny. I asked Him for a best friend, who I thought would be a female, and He had other plans in mind. All I can say is that when you know, you know. I hear of people getting married after meeting for only a couple weeks, and all I say again is that when you know you know.

To say we were inseparable would be a huge understatement! We were seeing each other every day. The Sunday after our first date he invited me to meet his family. I fell in love with each and every one of them. His mom was the choir director of our church, so she quickly added me to the roster. Little did I know that his family had been scheming to try and get us together all summer long. I think a few prayers were said on our behalf as well. Me and his mom were becoming very quick friends. Remember my list and the part about music? Well his mom played the piano and sang so I got to check music off my list. God is funny that way.

My mom mentioned to me that we were seeing each other entirely too much so she suggested that we hang out on weekends and see each other only a couple days a week. My mom knew what she was talking about. She said that she didn't want us to smother each other. I agreed with her and thought it to be great advice. It made us miss each other and made us even more appreciative of each other when we did hang out.

I was going back to college the following month. I knew that was going to be extremely hard, and it was. We took full advantage of every moment we had together

and made the most of it. One day my cousin called and asked where I was, and my mom told her we were out looking for tile. Yeah, those are the kind of things we did. We both enjoyed looking at houses and talking about our dream homes. We got along so well and if I can give you a little advice, if you are working so hard on a relationship you are in, you shouldn't have to. I tell people all the time that while we were dating it felt like we were on a raft, floating down a peaceful stream. Look for peace in a relationship. You have a lifetime with this person you choose. Make it a peaceful one.

LET'S REFLECT

I don't know if you are married or not. If you are, take this time to go back to when you first met your true love.

Remember… reminisce about your dating years. Remember the things you did, how you felt, the smells and beauty you witnessed together. Remember the sights and the way you felt. This was really good for me to remember what it was that first attracted me to him. That is why I'm still married to him after 24 years.

If you are not married and are looking for Mister Right, take the time right now and make your list. God placed me with a man who would read his list to me first. Not in my wildest dreams did I think that could happen. Don't make your list too long. Just make a list of the things you couldn't live without.

CHAPTER 3

Nuggets of Wisdom

Love is patient, love is kind. It does not envy, it does not boast, it is not proud. It does not dishonor others, it is not self-seeking, it is not easily angered, it keeps no record of wrongs, Love does not delight in evil but rejoices with the truth. It always protects, always trusts. always hopes, always perseveres.

1 COR. 13:4-6

I went back to college not sure if this relationship would last the distance. I was in Michigan at Calvin College, and he was in New Jersey. We were 12 hours away. I didn't tell him this at first but prior to meeting him I had dated a guy and we had a long-distance relationship as well. It lasted 14 days. So, do you see why I wasn't too confident that this one was going to last? It's all in the work you put in it. Greg tried to come up once every other month and we talked every day for hours sometimes. I'm not going to lie, having had this distance definitely has helped us throughout our marriage. I guess because we had no choice but to get to know each other because we talked to each other instead of being physical for most of our dating relationship.

After a year of the back and forth, we both couldn't take it any longer. I decided to move back home. It was so nice being back home. I knew we would eventually get married, and I had missed him so much! We survived our nine-month long distance relationship, and it wasn't always easy. It was hard going a month or a couple months without seeing him, but throughout that time we had gotten to know each other very well because we talked every night. It was so nice to date and see each other whenever we wanted to.

I hadn't been home long when he started talking about marriage, which freaked me out a little. It made me very nervous because my mom had been divorced, and I had many people in my family that had gotten divorced. His parents were happily married, and I loved being around his family. They were such a wonderful example of what I wanted. I mostly admired that at dinner, without fail, they would read a devotional after everyone had finished eating. It was read out of *Our Daily Bread,* a devotional our church always provided to the congregation monthly. No one could leave the table until they thanked the Lord and ended their meal with a prayer of thanks. They always started a meal with prayer and ended their meal with prayer, and I loved that! Our family dinners were much different, and I was definitely learning some great habits for the future with our family. I still didn't feel ready to get married, and the thought about marriage scared me.

I prayed a lot about my fear of marriage and asked the Lord to take it away. One day I woke up and all my fear was gone. I can't explain it. I was so ready to get married that it's all I thought about. After our little conversation about marriage, where I freaked out because he bought up the 'marriage' word, he wouldn't bring it up anymore. Now I was so ready, and it was driving me crazy that he wouldn't propose. This is just silly me, but I took off a ring that I always wore on my ring finger and decided to make room just in case. One day we were sitting at

Tricia DeBoer

church, and he was holding my hand and he noticed I had taken that ring off. I kind of *shyishly* (if that's even a word) said, "I think my finger needs a new ring; it looks a little naked." I said it with a big smile on my face. He just held my hand with a big smile on his face.

It didn't take too long after that until he proposed. He came over and asked my mom if it was okay to marry her daughter—this conversation happened while I was getting ready in my room, and I didn't even know it. When I came downstairs from my room, my cousin from next door was over and everybody had a big grin on their faces. I knew something was up. We ended up going to our favorite restaurant, Mt. Fuji. To get there you had to drive up a steep hill, and when you got to the top, it overlooked New York City and New Jersey. It was such a beautiful view.

Dinner was delicious as always. We loved the hibachi shrimp and steak, which we ordered every time. The chef made a heart out of the rice, which was so cute. Then we walked to the car, it was drizzling that night. We got to the car, he opened my door, and then he said, "I forgot something."

So, I said to go get it.

Then he said, "Will you marry me?"

I know there were other things that he said, but I was too busy squealing with excitement! "Yes, yes! Of course I will marry you!" It felt so surreal looking at my finger with this beautiful ring on it! I was ecstatic! That night I fell asleep with a huge smile on my face. I woke up forgetting that anything happened, until I saw my ring and said, "Oh, yeah. I got engaged!"

Going to church the next day was just as fun because I wouldn't tell anyone, I just wanted them to notice the ring and squeal with excitement as I did. Everyone was so happy for us.

The pastor and his wife kept giving us hugs, and by the time we left the church, I think the whole congregation knew.

It was at that church that we got married and Pastor Kuiken, who we love and adore, was the pastor who married us. We had a beautiful ceremony where my three-year-old niece sang the most adorable solo. I also sang a song as the congregation had their eyes closed. My husband opened his eyes and was very surprised to see me singing. It was a sweet moment. The wedding went by so fast. It was all so beautiful. We had five bridesmaids and a maid of honor as well as five groomsmen and a best man. We also had two junior bride's maids and a ring bearer (who was my nephew, and he just got married) as well as the cutest little flower girl (who is now married with three children). Wow does time fly!

We are going into our twenty-fifth year of marriage this year. Sometimes it feels like we just got married yesterday. Writing all this down is definitely taking me down a beautiful memory lane. I also just took out my wedding album to savor the moment.

For our honeymoon, we went to Fort Lauderdale, Florida, stayed a couple days at a hotel on the beach, and left on a cruise to the Bahamas a few days later. At least that's what was supposed to happen. When we got off the plane in Florida, we went to try to rent a car. Since we got married a little young (I was 23 and he was 24) no one would let us rent a car because of our age.

At the time, we gave our licenses and credit card to the Hertz salesperson, unbeknownst to us, he had dropped our credit card on the floor and handed Greg our driver's licenses. Then we went looking for a taxi. At that time, we realized that our credit card was missing, and we looked all over and couldn't find it. Thankfully my mom, when we were leaving, gave me a twenty-dollar bill that I reluctantly received from her because I felt like we had plenty of money and didn't need any. Thankfully I had that or else we would have had to walk to our hotel.

When we got to the hotel, thankfully it was all prepaid, but we had no money to eat anywhere, and we were starving. There was another credit card that my husband had that never worked anywhere, but we tried to use it. When we were dating, we tried to use it on a few dates and it never worked, but God! Here is where we started seeing His mighty hand on our marriage. We handed the hotel clerk that credit card that never worked and asked her if she could use this card to prepay for dinners at the hotel. Can you believe it worked? So, the only place we could eat was at the restaurant within the hotel. We were ecstatic and ate like pigs.

The next day my mom wired us some of our wedding money, enough to survive on. Remember the twenty dollars my mom gave me? Well, the taxi cost seventeen dollars and some change so all I had left was less than three dollars. We had thankfully packed our roller blades. (Once again you may have to google roller blades. They were sort of like roller skates, but the wheels were in a straight line with a stopper on the back.) Anyway, we had to rollerblade into town in 100-degree heat because we didn't have enough money for a taxi. It was grueling. The Western Union was a few miles away, and I thought I was going to die before I saw a cent of that money. I went into Subway and begged for a tall cup of ice and water, and they were kind enough to only charge me for one. That was just the beginning of our adventurous honeymoon.

The next day our cruise was leaving the port at 6:30 a.m. so we left really early so that we wouldn't miss the boat. When we got to the port it was like I was watching a movie. Our boat was already taking off! "What in the world!" I yelled. I couldn't believe my very eyes. I thought to myself that we could take a running leap and maybe we could make it in the boat. I shared my adventurous thought with my husband, and he looked at me and said, "With bags and all, you really think we will make it? We don't have wings." I was devastated, to say the least.

Then I remembered that before we left the hotel I was sitting on my suitcase because it was 5:30 a.m. and I could barely stand up because I was so tired. I was looking out to the ocean and for the first time I saw waves. The past few days the ocean had looked like a lake. I said, "Lord if I am going to get sick because of choppy waves on the boat I'd rather not go on it." God heard my prayer and answered it.

Come to find out, there were two cruise ships that were supposed to go to Bahamas. At some point, they dry docked one, which was our ship, and we never received our new ticket in the mail with its new departure time. This took place in 1994, way before cell phones, email, and internet.

We ended up taking a small jet to the Bahamas. It was such a fun time, and we were there in thirty minutes. God is so good all the time!

This is how great God is: On our way back from Bahamas we were able to take our cruise ship back. We ran into the sweetest, funniest couple that told us all about their experience on the boat going to the Bahamas. They said that the waves were so big, and the boat was moving up and down so much that so many people were getting sick that the crew was passing out plastic bags to everyone. *Thank you, Jesus, for hearing this tired girl's prayer!* I would have been so miserable!

After we got back from the Bahamas, our new credit card had come in the mail and we were ready for the next part of our honeymoon, which was Vail, Colorado. When we first talked about where we wanted to go on our honeymoon, I, of course, said Hawaii. My husband, who loves the mountains, said Colorado. So, to compromise and to go to both the beach and mountains we had to go with a cheaper destination to enjoy a beach.

Colorado was so fun. I'm so thankful that me and my husband are opposites. He brings me on new adventures that I would never have experienced without him, like rock climbing and mountain biking. I bring him out of his box by making him go to Europe because I love to travel and want to see the world. We really balance each other out quite nicely.

Once we got back home from our honeymoon a couple weeks later, we packed all of our belongings and moved to South Carolina. It was a bit scary to move to a new city and state, but we were up for the challenge.

I may have forgotten to mention that, six months prior to us getting married, Greg was given an opportunity to work in construction with his brother-in-law who had just started his own company, so he moved to South Carolina. This could be what brought on my panic attack that happened at the church (planning a wedding for 400 people didn't help either), which I will go into more detail about later. Since he was working, I was going bonkers staying home by myself with nothing to do and not knowing anybody except for Greg's sister and her husband. She had a full-time job, so I didn't see her much.

The very next day I had a job at a daycare. I had to get out of the apartment because the walls felt like they were closing in on me. I loved my first daycare job. I was working at a daycare back in New Jersey, and I missed being around two-year-olds and their cute smiling faces. I was still a bit lonely and homesick, but having this job definitely kept my mind too occupied to dwell on it.

There was another God moment that I have to share. If anyone is married or in a relationship this will be really helpful. I was at my sister-in-law's hanging out with a bunch of his family. My husband is one of five, including himself, and at the time three out of the four siblings lived within driving distance from us, so we saw each other quite frequently. Well, to this day I do not remember what caused me to get to this point, but I had become very mad at my husband. I don't remember what he did or didn't do. I was so livid, and we were all getting into our cars to celebrate my in-law's wedding anniversary at a nearby restaurant. I didn't want to get in the car with him, I didn't want to drive with him anywhere, and more than anything, I didn't want to go sit in a restaurant and pretend there was nothing wrong, so I refused to get in the car.

Now, just a side note, this is not my personality at all. I'm normally a go with the flow, pretty chill person. I just stood outside of the car thinking, *What should I do? Should I ask him to take me home?* Then I decided to go to the bathroom to think about some more options of what to do. While I was in the bathroom, I thought about a book I read before I got married called *Fit to Be Tied*, by Bill and Lynne Hybels. The book is about their marriage and their struggles in their marriage because they got married at 18 years old. (Here is a little advice, if you are that young and want to get married, try and wait until you at least turn 21. I promise that you become a different person from 18 to 21.) In the book, it talks about how one of them was so angry at the other and it was not ending, and she was just getting madder and madder. She said that she removed herself from the situation and went to the bathroom. She began to pray that the Lord would take her anger away and that He would take away her pride. She didn't feel much different, but when she got out of the bathroom, she was not mad anymore.

I thought to myself that it was worth a try, so I prayed to the Lord and asked Him to please take away my pride. That's all I could muster out. I walked out of the bathroom, and like the book, not feeling any different. I went to the car to see my husband waiting for me in the driver's seat. He said, "Do you want me to take you home?"

You may not believe this, but I said, "What are you talking about? I thought we were going to the restaurant?" Would you believe that God made me completely forget what I was angry about?

My husband was shocked, and I was thinking, *Let's go! Everyone is waiting for us.*

I just brought this up to him last night because I wanted to make sure I got his permission to write about this. He asked me if I remembered what I was so mad about, and still to this day I have no clue. God is amazing! I'm just so thankful for His love and that He gets us. He knows our needs, desires, and wants. When we ask Him with a pure heart, He answers. He may not answer us the way we want Him to answer, but He knows what's best for us and He always answers, sometimes with a "yes," sometimes with a "no," and sometimes with a "not now, but later."

I ended up sharing this experience with my young married group at a church that we were attending at the time. After I shared that God just made all of my hurt, anger, and all of the awful feelings disappear I had a few couples thank me for sharing. A few Sundays later a couple wanted to share something that was on their hearts. The wife shared how one night she had gotten home, and her husband had made her so mad that they were in a yelling screaming fight. She proceeded to share with us about how in the middle of her anger she started recalling the experience we shared the other Sunday, about how God just made my anger disappear. Right after she remembered, she got on her knees and started to pray. Soon after, her husband joined her on the floor and started praying right next to her.

Can we just take a moment and ponder how beautiful this scene must have been? Two people are yelling at each other saying who knows what, and the wife drops to her knees to pray, and the husband does the same. All because they chose to ask God to take away their pride. Wow! How amazing is God? He only asks us to come to Him and lay our burdens down and He does the rest. He takes our yolk and makes it easier for us. We serve an amazing God!

Many people have asked me what has helped my husband and I to stay married for 25 years. I always let them know that we have definitely had our ups and downs, but marriage takes work. It's not going to be a bed of roses all the time. You have to choose to love this person—faults and all. I didn't say you have to love the faults. The most important thing you can do for yourself in choosing your lifetime spouse is to choose someone whose faults you can live with. None of us are perfect and we can't expect our spouse to be either.

When I was dating, I always looked for "deal breakers." If I met someone and they had a personality that I could not live with, it was a deal breaker for me. That means if I couldn't live with their faults, it was not worth dating them anymore or at all, so I would break it off or not even go on a date with them.

I only had three long relationships in my life. One was my sophomore year of high school that lasted five months, the other was my senior year that lasted seven months, and we broke up once I was in college because I knew he was not my future husband, and I didn't want to hold on to a relationship I knew wasn't going anywhere. The longest was a year and a half and then Greg proposed to me. Other than those three, my dating consisted of one with very few second dates.

I believed that, if the feelings weren't there or I saw a deal breaker on the first date, then why waste my time and why make him waste his time? And I would tell them just like that. I had many guys who thanked me for not stringing them along, and I had others that asked me to give them more time. I didn't need more time. The funny thing is that my husband's dating life looked a lot like mine.

There are three things I always tell people when they ask me how I've been married this long. My first nugget of wisdom is to *find someone who challenges your mind.* This is what I mean: My husband will talk to me about pistons and car parts. I used to have no idea what any of that meant, but now I do. Although I wouldn't know where to begin to fix a car, he has explained car parts and what their uses are to the point that now I'm starting to get it. It's not a conversation that would normally interest me, but it's new knowledge that I can gain that is now interesting and useful to me. My son loves to pretend he is fixing cars like his daddy. So, he challenges his mind also.

Second, you need to *learn to lean and lead each other.* I have leaned on him for so many things, but he has also leaned on me when he has needed it. Although I believe, and it's biblical, that the man should be the head of the household, there are areas where I may understand more, and I encourage him and teach him some things.

The third, and it pertains mostly to once you're married, is to *go on dates once a week.* This has been a lot more difficult with our son because it's harder now to find a babysitter or we feel like we shouldn't spend the money. The first thing our pastor who married us said at our first marriage counseling session was to go on a date together once a week. He has six kids, so if he could make it happen so can we. I always remember how he said he always squeezed in a date a week no matter what. Now I see why it's so important. When you don't spend that quality time away alone, you may forget all the fun you both have when you're together.

I realized this one time when my poor husband got a canker sore in his throat, and it grew to be as big as a golf ball. That was not fun for him or me. He could only eat chicken soup for nearly a month. He couldn't have anything spicy or too tasty because it would burn his throat. He was miserable. I was miserable. I remember going to God and asking Him to take it away and help us with our marriage because we were feeling very distant from each other. The next day God reminded me that we hadn't gone on a date for at least a month or two. That weekend I made him go on a date with me. We had such a good time. We held hands, laughed, and we felt so much more connected. The date reminded me of how much fun we have together. When you don't date, you can really become like two ships at sea. Although dating looks very different with our son, we still try to be intentional about dating at least every other week. After twenty-five years we still make each other laugh, we hold each other's hands, and we have a lot of fun together.

The fourth nugget of wisdom is that we *allow each other girl time for me and guy time for him*. This one is also so important because when you are with each other all the time, we don't allow our individuality to flourish. I'm a people person so I love to hang out with my friends, and I need it. It makes me happy, and I feel more myself after spending some good quality time with a friend or a bunch of girlfriends. Although my husband is completely opposite of me because he's more of a homebody, he still benefits from having guy time, laughing, and getting his mind off stressful things like work. This has really helped our marriage a lot. After hanging out with friends or taking a road trip with my girls, I feel refreshed and excited to be back with my sweet little family. I hope these help you. They certainly have been vital in making our marriage work.

LET'S REFLECT

I shared a lot in this chapter about what has helped me in *my* marriage. Take a moment and write down what your nuggets of wisdom are that you would share if someone were to ask you what makes *your* marriage work.

If you are not married, then ask yourself what nuggets of wisdom you feel would be important for you when you do get married.

If you are in a difficult marriage, ask yourself what nuggets of the ones I shared could you benefit from if you implemented them in your marriage or which one(s) do you need to work on in your marriage.

If you need to date more, then be intentional about making it happen. Don't be surprised if you go on a date and you argue and it's not a great date, but don't give up. Your next one will be better. Keep working on your marriage. It's worth it!

CHAPTER 4

Three Fuzzy Pillows

For he will command his angels concerning you
to guard you in all your ways; they will lift you up
in their hands, so that you will not strike your foot
against a stone.

PSALM 91:11-12

Like I said before, after I had moved to South Carolina, I had been a bit stir crazy being stuck in my apartment by myself while my hubby was at work. I'm not very good at staying home alone with no one to talk to. By the next day I had gotten a job at a daycare. I was so excited to get to know some new people because I was a bit homesick at this time. If I'm being honest, we had considered moving back a few times. My husband kept saying that this was a "great place to bring up kids" and "we have better weather here."

I really enjoyed being at the daycare, and I had made a few really good friends. I was also asked by a Christian school to help them out because they needed a Spanish teacher for their first through fifth graders. Their Spanish teacher had gotten ill, and they needed a quick replacement. I felt bad because the school was put in this predicament, so I interviewed and got the job. I loved teaching Spanish, and the kids were so fun. In total, I had 130 kids that I was teaching Spanish. I loved teaching Spanish, but I was also working my full-time job at the daycare. I don't know how I did it, looking back. During lunch and nap time for my two-year-old class I would run to the Christian school down the road, which luckily was only 10 minutes away from the daycare. I would teach Spanish for a couple hours and run back to my two-year-old class and get there right when they were getting up from their nap.

To add one more thing to my life, I decided to sell makeup on the side as well. *What was I thinking?* One day I was on my way to pick up some make up at my director's house for a customer. It was on a Saturday, and I was driving my mom and aunt around and we were running some errands. As I was driving, it started to rain. I heard three raindrops fall on the hood of my car. It wasn't the normal sound of raindrops. The sound is very hard to explain. It was more like a soft thump. I didn't think much about it. As I was driving, I was approaching a yellow light and decided to run through it. I was driving alongside a semi-truck who I thought was going to run the yellow light as well.

Here is where the story gets a little weird. All of a sudden, I heard an audible voice that said, "Hold on to the steering wheel and close your eyes." Most of you reading this would have said, "No way." But let me explain to you: It was like I was a robot that didn't have the function button for 'no.' I peacefully just did what the voice was telling me to do. The next thing I know, I am above my car looking down into it. I didn't feel myself fly out of the car I just all of a sudden could see into my car as if it had no hood. Another strange thing is that it was only me in my car. I didn't see my mom or my aunt. Then, as I looked closer to where I was sitting, I saw three fuzzy white pillows surrounding me. I had one on my left, one on my right, and one right in front of me.

The next thing I knew I was back in my car. Once I was in the car it was spinning really fast. I told myself, *Okay, I've been on a ride at Great Adventure in New Jersey that felt like this. It was called the "Rotter Rooter." I can handle this.* Then, we stopped spinning and my car peacefully stopped and was lifted up onto the curb.

Once we stopped, I opened my eyes and my aunt in the passenger's seat said, "Did you hear the explosion?" I told her that I hadn't heard anything. Then I asked if she was okay. She let me know that she was. All of a sudden, I heard a strange moaning behind me. I turned around, and my mom was covered in blood and not able to talk. I started to freak out and had to turn back around before I passed out. I asked her if she was okay and all she could do was moan. I started to pray that my mom was not hurt as badly as she looked and that she would be okay.

My heart was palpitating so fast, and I was starting to have a panic attack. I quickly tried to open my car door, but it wouldn't open. I asked my aunt to try to open her door and hers wouldn't open either! Then I remembered that I had manual windows that I could roll down myself. (When you are in a situation like this, you forget everything—at least I did.) Then I started rolling my window down as fast as I could to get out of there. I finally made it out and was very lightheaded and could barely stand. All I could do was lay on the front window of my car so that I wouldn't pass out, and I prayed again. I said, "Lord, please let my mom survive and bring an ambulance to us soon!" Then I just laid there with my eyes closed. We didn't have cell phones then so all I could do was pray. I wasn't able to walk because of my panic attack, and I had no idea where the nearest gas station was.

Can I just say that God is so good, because moments—not seconds but moments—later I felt someone touching my arm, and I opened my eyes. Three cars had stopped, and they had parked all around my car. I saw three people that had black tee-shirts that said EMS on the front. I don't know if they were on their way to work or back from work, but at that moment I didn't care where they were coming from. I was just so glad they were there. Two of them were already trying to help my mom, and one showed up by my side and asked me if I was okay. I told her I was okay, just having a panic attack, and I was so happy they were there! She told me that the ambulance was on their way.

By this time, we were surrounded by people who had stopped by my car and were trying to help. I was overhearing a conversation in the distance and they were talking about what they had seen. So, what I can recall from the conversation, a yellow Cadillac hit my car on my side, which caused it to spin. Then my car hit a telephone pole and we ricocheted off the pole and started to spin the other way. Then my car stopped and looked like it was lifted and placed on the curb. I then realized that I was lifted out of my car for God to show me that He was taking care of me and keeping me from getting hurt. He then placed me back in the car when we had bounced off the telephone pole and were spinning. *Only God!* I'm seriously taking a moment for myself to glorify Him as I relive this accident. What a mighty God we serve!

A stranger that had stopped kindly called my husband to let him know, and Greg came quickly. The ambulance had taken my mom and aunt to a nearby hospital, and I was left behind waiting for my husband. As I stood there alone walking around, I just thanked my heavenly Father for everything. For my angels He surrounded me with that allowed me to still be alive throughout this whole accident with not a scratch on me. Not one bruise or cut—nothing!

Tricia DeBoer

My aunt was okay. She just had a little whiplash. My mom, thank the Lord for His mighty provision, survived, too. She ended up with three broken ribs, a broken collar bone, her nose was cut open, which was the reason for all the blood, and she almost bit her tongue off. She didn't have her seat belt on, so unfortunately, she was bounced around all over the place during the accident.

My husband came soon after and walked around the scene with me in awe like I was in awe. Then I remembered the rain drops that dropped in my car. Those must have been the three angels that surrounded me. I then noticed that my car door was dented in a foot right where I was sitting, but, once again, not a bruise. The passenger's door was also dented in about a foot, and also not a bruise on my aunt. *Isn't God good?* Although my mom was pretty bruised up, she survived. So once again, *isn't God good?*

A few months after the accident while I was working in the daycare, I started to feel very faint. I quickly got someone to watch my class and ran outside to get some fresh air. I felt like I was about to pass out, so I sat on the ground and leaned against a wall. My dizzy feeling was not going away. The feeling got worse and worse. It got to the point that I couldn't move because I felt like I was going to pass out, and I was feeling weaker and weaker. I thought that my time was coming to an end and that I was going to die. I looked out in front of me and actually said to myself, *If my time is now, at least I can die peacefully on a beautiful sunny day.*

At that moment, an employee was leaving for the day and was walking out the door to go home. She noticed that I was leaned up against the wall, so she came over by me. I told her I was faint and asked her to call my mom to pick me up. She was so kind and did as I asked. My mom came quickly because she was so worried, and she didn't live very far from the daycare. My coworker stayed until my mom came and she had to carry me into the car. My mom took me home and I slept the rest of the day.

The following day I made an appointment with a doctor to see what was wrong with me. I didn't go to the doctor much, so I just went to a doctor I found across the street from where I worked. He said I had chronic fatigue and gave me a prescription for Prozac. I ended up not taking the Prozac. I had heard many things about it that made me uncomfortable. I just asked the Lord to heal me.

I can't paint a pretty picture, but the next few months were not fun at all. I didn't want to leave the house. I was very weak, and I stayed away from all my friends because I didn't have the energy to even laugh. I would get up or eat, and I took naps all day. With the way I was feeling, I couldn't go back to work, so I quit both the daycare and my part time Spanish teacher position. My panic attacks were so bad that I couldn't go to amusement parks or the mall for over four years.

I remember laying on the couch and asking God why this happened to me. I asked Him why I was alive if I couldn't even laugh or be myself anymore? I went to church on Sundays holding the walls because I was so afraid that I was going to pass out. My doctor had also told me that the best thing I could do for myself was to find a desk job, one that was not too stressful. I couldn't even walk to the next mailbox without someone holding me let alone be at a job all day. I thought I was going to live the rest of my life this way. I even went to New Jersey to visit family and all my cousins came to visit me because they were afraid that I was dying.

Tricia DeBoer

One day my sweet Aunt Rosa decided to make it her mission to get me better. I was living with my mom and her two sisters at the time, thankfully. This is the aunt who was in the passenger's seat during my accident. She told me that she hated seeing me this way, and she also told me that we were going to take small walks outside every day, even if it was just to the next mailbox. She said this was not the real me. I was usually smiling and full of life. I am a lot like my aunt. We have very similar personalities. She passed away just last year, and I will be forever grateful for what she did for me that summer. Walking every day is literally what caused me to get on my journey of healing.

I mentioned before that I almost passed out at church before my wedding. I was diagnosed with mitral valve prolapse. I was still taking medication for my panic attacks, and it just didn't seem to be working anymore. I was tired of taking drugs that altered my mood and my personality. I told the Lord that I didn't want to take them anymore. I went to my cardiologist and told him how I felt about wanting to be done with drugs altogether. He told me the strangest thing. He said, "If you walk every day you can wean yourself off the medicine."

I started feeling much better because I was walking every day. The bouts of panic attacks still reared their ugly heads here and there, but I was learning how to deal with them. My new confidence had me feeling well enough to find a job and get out of the house. I was starting to feel a little stir crazy being at the house all this time. I had walked every day with my aunt, rain or shine. I started to walk a couple miles a day.

The walking and Jesus did wonders for me in so many ways. A realization came to me from walking so much. As I was walking around different places that caused me panic attacks, like church and the mall, I would tell myself that I have walked much further than this on my daily walks, and that I was not going to pass out. Even if I do, someone I am with will just pick me up and I will continue walking.

One of my greatest fears was going to the mall. I hadn't gone to one in about six months. I decided to go to the mall with my sweet, patient husband, and it felt like such a setback. My panic attacks were so severe there. He would encourage me to try to walk to the next bench I saw then we would sit down and take a break. That is what we did. He held my hand and encouraged me the whole time. What a guy!

It wasn't right away that everything was normal, but I realized that the more I faced my fears, the better I felt and the less panic attacks I would have. I knew I was on the way to normalcy; it was just going to take a little more time.

LET'S REFLECT

There is so much I am sharing about my private life. I feel very vulnerable right now, but the Lord told me to share my experiences because someone may need some encouragement or some hope.

What are you going through right now that you need hope for? Is it a sickness? Is it a hopeless situation? Talk to God right now. Let Him know how you feel. Ask Him what are your next steps.

What can you do today to make a step forward? Do you need to take a walk to the next mailbox? It wasn't easy for me, but I asked for God's help every day.

Take a moment to talk to God. He is right there waiting for you.

Tricia DeBoer

CHAPTER 5

The Blonde Lady
at the Door

For the Spirit God gave us does not make us timid,
but gives us power, love and self-discipline.

2 TIMOTHY 1:7

My job search had begun, and I had been praying for God to lead me to my next destination He wanted me to be. I was starting to feel much better, so it was time to look for an office job. I don't even remember how I heard about this job, but it was definitely my next assignment. Life's a journey. You may not realize the spirit's direction at the time, but when you look back, you can see the path He wanted you to follow.

It was the day of my interview at a pager company. (Pagers were a form of communication back in 2001 before cell phones came out. You may want to look it up and get a good laugh.) I walked into my interview and met the sweetest person who was soon to be my manager. The moment I sat down and she introduced herself, I knew we were going to be friends. We even had some mutual friends. I won't keep you waiting. I was hired on the spot.

This job was probably one of my favorites. The next step in my journey of life was meeting my manager. She told me in the interview that they prayed every morning and that she hoped I wouldn't mind. *Are you kidding me?* I thought to myself, *I think I'm going to love this job!* I picked up everything she taught me really fast, and my manager and I became the best of friends. I ended up working there for five years. God taught me so much through her during that time.

My first day at this new job was pretty amazing. We started our day with a beautiful prayer. She also ended her prayer every morning reminding us that we may be the only Jesus these customers may see. It started our day off on the right foot praying this way every morning. I loved our morning prayers.

There was something so different about this manager/new best friend. She was so bold when she talked about Jesus. She would talk about Jesus to just about everybody who walked through the door.

One day, these two big, tall guys walked into the store. They walked up to my manager, who we will call Amy, said, "Hey, Amy! How are you doing?" and gave her a big hug.

She responded. "I'm doing great! You boys going to church yet?"

I thought to myself, *Well that's a little forward.* She was not done.

The guys said, "Oh, Amy. We just got out yesterday, Grandma's already asking us to go."

She then proceeded to say, "You know you need Jesus, and you can't be half pregnant. You either love Jesus or you don't!"

I was floored. *Did she really just say that to these guys who tower over her about two feet?* Man, she was bold. *I would never be able to say that,* I thought to myself. I soon found out after they left that they had just gotten out of prison and Amy had known them for a long time. That was just one of her conversations, but she had many more of them.

She amazed me by how bold she was. I needed some of that! A few days later, she asked me to go to her church because her dad was the pastor and she wanted me to meet him. That week on a Wednesday night we went to her church. I expected a bigger church with lots of people, but it was completely the opposite. It was a quaint little church with no more than just twenty people. They played old southern gospel music, which was very new to me, but I enjoyed it. The people there were the kindest people I have ever met. I was greeted by hugs, and they all said they were so happy to have me there. Then we sat down, and Amy's dad began to preach, and preach he did. That sermon was as if he had been a fly on the wall in my home for years. Everything I was dealing with at the time was talked about with scripture included. I thought to myself, *Does he know me? Did God tell him about me?* I think I wrote five pages of notes that night.

At the end of the church service, he would call anyone who needed prayer to come up to the altar for him to pray for them. Then as I kept watching people walk up to the front, I noticed that as he prayed some of them would fall backwards. That was all new to me. At first it freaked me out, and then it intrigued me. There were at least ten people that walked up to the front, and seven had fallen to the floor. I had so many questions for Amy. I wanted to know what all that was about.

After the service was done, I finally met her dad. He greeted me with a hug and said, "Thank you for coming. How did you enjoy the service?" I told him that I really enjoyed it, and then I asked him how he knew so much about me without knowing me. He let me know that he didn't know anything about me, and that the Spirit had just led him to preach that sermon. Then he said, "I'm glad the Spirit spoke to you. It was so great meeting you. I hope you come again." I went every Wednesday and some Sundays for five years. That church and pastor had left quite an impression on me from the first day I visited.

I learned so many things going to that little church. One thing I really enjoyed was that they spoke about the Holy Spirit so freely. I had been to a lot of churches up to that point, but none spoke about the Holy Spirit like this one did.

My friend Amy explained to me why some people fell down after her dad prayed for them. She said it was called being slain in the Spirit. It was a moment that just you and God have. He may speak to you, you may get answers for something, or you may just lay there and feel really peaceful. I was still scared about it all and didn't know if I would ever do it. It was all so different to me, but I was definitely curious.

I started thinking a lot about walking to the front and getting prayed for. When he would end the service and call people up for prayer, I always wanted to walk up to the front but then I would be too scared and chicken out. I thought to myself, *What would happen if I get prayed over and I fell down and no one would catch me?* Satan can get in your head so easily and that's exactly what he was doing to me. You know when people say, "I'm just in my head right now"? Nine out of ten times, I bet you it's Satan messing with them.

One night I had a dream. In my dream, I had walked up to the front of the church to get prayed for and when I fell backwards, it felt like I was falling into a soft cloud, and then I woke up. That week or the week after, I finally did it. I went to church that Wednesday night, sat in my usual seat and enjoyed the sermon. When he was done preaching, he said, "Anyone who is in need of prayer, please come to the front. I would love to pray with you." My heart was beating so fast, and before I knew what I was doing, I was walking up to the front. It was finally my turn, and the pastor said, "What can I pray for you, sweetie?" I forget what I was prayed over for it's been so long ago, but all I remember is that as I was falling backwards it felt like I was falling into a soft cloud, just like in my dream. As I was laying on the ground I felt so peaceful. It was a special time with me and God. It felt like no one else was in the room, just me and Him.

I couldn't believe it had taken me two years to finally do it. The next few days some strange things started to happen. (Just a side note: everyone's experience will be different, but I feel like the Lord wants me to share mine.) The following day I felt like I had an extra spring in my step. I felt bolder and more courageous. Things that I had shied away from, I wanted to confront.

If that wasn't strange enough, one day I was driving to my manager's house, and as I was driving, I saw a vision of me walking into her house. As I was opening her screened door, my cell phone rang and it was a close friend of mine calling. Then as quickly as it came, the vision left. I got to my friend's house about five minutes later. I walked up her steps and you guessed it, my cell phone rang. I didn't even have to see who it was. I knew it was my friend calling from out of town.

God was just starting to teach me how He was going to be communicating to me in the future. I was still a little confused by it all. I shared my experience with Amy, and she was the least shocked about it. She said she had similar things happen to her. It was what she called "Holy Spirit promptings."

There was something else that Amy was doing that had me very intrigued. She would speak in her prayer language, as she called it. One day, I woke up very sick and I called her to let her know I was not going to be going to work that day. I was nauseous and had no energy. She told me that my other co-worker that worked the front desk with me had called out sick before me. I was so upset. She said come to work and I will lay hands on you and pray for you. I was not happy about having to come to work at all.

I made it to work, but almost had to pull over to the side of the road because I felt so sick. When I got to work, I let her know that I was not happy to be there. She said, "I know, I know. You're mad that I made you come in. Come in my office so that I can pray for you." I had no faith in her praying for me. I had such a bad attitude, and I didn't even care if she prayed for me.

She had me sit back in her chair and she placed her hands on my stomach. She proceeded to pray in her prayer language. I don't know what she was saying because it was a language I couldn't understand. All I know is right where she had placed her hands my stomach started to feel numb. She finished the prayer and then looked at me and said, "How do you feel?" You may not believe what I am about to tell you, but I felt like I had never been sick. I felt perfectly fine!

Now my curiosity was peaked. We spent most of the day talking about what had just happened. She explained to me that she had the gift of healing. She explained that God gives you many gifts. It's up to Him which ones He gives to each person. I kept telling her that I wanted that same gift and she said, "It's not what *you* want. It's what God wants for you, baby girl." It's all I thought about that day. I couldn't wait to go to church to visit the pastor and ask him all my questions.

I ended up going to church that week and went to the front to get prayed for. I was on the floor waiting with others who had gotten slain in the spirit as well, and the strangest thing happened. A lady who I know but was not close friends with moved over closer to me and said these exact words, "You have your prayer language, and the Lord has asked me to stay by your side until you receive it." I'm not going to lie, I almost passed out I was so shocked at what she had said. *Was she reading my mind? How did she know?* I thought to myself. Later she explained to me that the Holy Spirit had led her to me to help me in receiving my prayer language.

As she sat next to me, she had me repeat a couple of syllables, the ones that just came to my mind. I don't remember what they were because this was such a long time ago. All I remember is that this odd language started to come out of me. A language I had never even heard before. She also explained to me that when I spoke it sometimes the Lord would let me know a little about what I was speaking and other times He would not. She also told me that we were His vessels, and He would speak through us.

I could not believe what had just happened. I was elated to say the least. The lady had also said that she had even prayed over her washing machine, and it started working again. *What in the world? Her washing machine?* As I drove home, I started singing in my prayer language, I felt like I was singing about how beautiful nature is and how beautiful God's creation is. It was all so strange, but at the same time so peaceful.

One day that week I was asked to close the store by myself, and I was not excited about it. Everyone was out of town and my manager had to leave early so I had to do it. That morning, I felt like I needed to bring this extra couple's devotional book that I had to work with me. I thought it was a little odd, but I grabbed it and took it with me. The day went by pretty quickly because we were very busy that day. Everyone had left the office and I was all alone at my desk. It was probably around 5:45 pm. As I sat at my desk, I started to see a vision. A lady with blonde curly hair walked up to the front door, I let her in, she sat at my desk, I grabbed her hands and prayed in my prayer language with her. Then the vision was gone. I didn't think much about it. It was six o'clock and I was shutting the door as quickly as I could, I couldn't wait for my day to be over. I thought to myself, *Oh, well. No lady.*

After locking the door, I sat down and started my closing procedures when all of a sudden, I heard a knock at the door. I looked up and it was a blonde lady with curly hair! *Oh, wow,* is what I thought to myself. So, I walked to the door and opened it and let her know that we closed at six, but I would help her out this time. She sat in the chair right in front of me. I helped her with what she needed, and then I boldly said, "Ma'am, I know you don't know me, but would you mind if I prayed for you?" She told me she would like that, and then I added "Do you mind if I pray in my prayer language?" Once again she said that it was okay. I held her hands just like in the vision and started to pray in my prayer language. I felt in my spirit that it had to do with her family, specifically her husband and son.

When I was done, she looked at me with wide eyes and said, "Do you know what you prayed over me?"

I let her know that the Holy Spirit just revealed to me that it was about her husband and son, but no details. She started to cry. I didn't ask any questions. I just reached in my bag and said, "I believe this is yours." And I handed her the couples devotional that I was led to bring in that morning.

As I handed it to her, she said, "Thank you so much!" Then I asked her if she went to church. She let me know that she hadn't been in five years. Then I said, "You need to go to church so that you can hear more from God and not just from total strangers at a store."

We both laughed, and she said she was going to start to go to church with the family very soon. She then gave me a big hug. I told her that I would be praying for her and her family.

LET'S REFLECT

I want you to think back of a time where you felt a little odd about doing something, and now you can look back and see God was all over it. Write about that experience. Perhaps God is recalling that time for you so that you can see for the first time that God's hand was in it all along.

If you can't think of a time, then are you being courageous in your walk with God? When was the last time you shared the gospel with anyone?

Make it a habit to ask God what He wants you to do with your day, and who He wants you to touch. Ask that He bring you those God appointments. You want to be used by God.

CHAPTER 6

You Will Have a Son

*You will conceive and give birth to a son, and you
are to call him Jesus.*

LUKE 1:31

In 2006, I started working at a bank right after coming back from a mission trip I took to Peru that changed my life. It was such a wonderful experience. We helped out at an orphanage in Cieneguilla, Peru. Every day we would have a delicious breakfast and take a bus that they called a "combie." Then we would drive to an orphanage that was ten minutes away. We were either assigned to play with the adorable children all day or we had to do some type of manual labor.

The first day I was assigned to the baby room. There was a preemie that wasn't more than five pounds. It was the tiniest baby I had ever seen. I think they had him in some doll clothes, at least it looked like it. I couldn't help myself… I held him all day. That little baby had no one to call "Mommy" or "Daddy," and it truly broke my heart thinking about it.

Before I left to go on my trip, my husband said, "Don't come home with a suitcase full of babies." He knows me too well. He knew I would fall in love with at least one of them and I would end up coming home with him or her. Although I enjoyed holding this baby, I didn't have an overwhelming feeling of bringing him home with me. Not with any of the children there.

Now, my friend was another story. When he set eyes on this one little boy, they were immediately drawn to each other. My friend couldn't get enough of him, and that boy was stuck to him like glue. It was the sweetest most special thing to watch. On our way back home, I asked my friend about the boy he fell in love with. He then told me he had two other siblings. I said, "Wow, your wife is going to freak out." We had a good laugh about it, and I told him that I would be praying for him and his wife and this decision. They had no children at the time. After four years, lots of waiting, frustration, and tears, the Lord blessed them, and they were able to adopt all three children. Walking through that special time with them gave me hope that one day I would be blessed with a child as well.

I had just gotten home from my incredible mission trip to Peru and the Lord was ready for my next assignment. I was hired right away by a bank that was an hour away from home. My husband said to take the job and eventually they would move me closer to home, so I took the job even though it was a very long commute. I met the most amazing people there, and it ended up being my new work home for two years. My manager who hired me took another position closer to home, two months after I started. The Lord blessed me with the sweetest, most caring manager. Let's just call her Mama Sue. I also called her mama because she treated all of us like we were her children. We all loved "Mama Sue."

One day very soon after I started working at this bank, a guy walked into my office. I asked him what he needed, and he said, "The strangest thing happened to me. I felt like I was supposed to turn into this driveway, and I parked my car and here I am."

So, I asked him if he had an account here, and he said that he didn't.

So, then I told him, "If you don't have an account here, the Lord drove you to my office because he has something for you." I proceeded to ask him if he went to church anywhere. He told me he hadn't been to church in a long time. Then, I said, "Maybe you need to start going to church because he sent you here to me because he knew I would tell you, son, you need to start going to church."

That was it. He said, "Yes ma'am," and left my office. I never saw him again.

Another day a gentleman walked into my office. He did have an account at the bank, but he had never been to Spartanburg, South Carolina. He was a pastor from Hawaii, and he was wearing a Hawaiian shirt. He was just the sweetest guy. I asked him what brought him to South Carolina, and he said he was attending a pastor's conference right up the road. After I helped him with what he needed, he asked me if he could pray for me. I said, "Of course." He then held both of my hands.

In mid-prayer he stopped and said, "Do you want a family?" I told him I was married but eventually we wanted children. He continued the prayer saying, "Lord, we thank you for her son."

I quickly interrupted him in mid-prayer and said, "Wait, what did you say?"

He then opened his eyes and looked me straight on and said, "You are going to have a son. You are not to ask God for a son. You are to thank God for your son."

That is all that I remember from his prayer. Everything else was a blur. It is all I thought of from that day forward.

How could God bring me a total stranger all the way from Hawaii to tell me those words? Let me explain. At that time, I was traveling internationally, domestically, all over the place. I wasn't thinking of having kids. I was too busy seeing the world. But that prayer did something to me. Those words were all I could think about.

I felt like what Mary, the mother of Jesus, must have felt. A stranger approached her and said, "You will have a son…" It was definitely a shocker to me as it must have been to her, and she was younger than I was at the time. I wonder if she knew that it was an angel in front of her bearing this news, or did she think it was a stranger that suddenly walked up to her like I did? I wonder if the following days those words were all that she thought about. I started to be able to relate to Mary. I wasn't thinking about having a child, and I really don't think that she was either. We both had to make a decision. Do we believe these words from a stranger? Whether I believed it or not, it was all that was consuming my mind.

A few years later, I was still working at the same bank but had transferred to a branch closer to home. One day this lady walked into my office. She was wearing a light purple sweat suit, she had short curly hair, and she had no teeth. She was a very sweet lady who praised Jesus the whole time she was in my office. Her love for Jesus was so evident and she spoke about her Lord with absolute reverence and passion for God. When I finished helping her with what she came in for she said, "Do you want kids?" I told her that I would love to have a baby one day. Then I asked her why she asked me that question, and she said, "Because I see a crib with many presents. You're going to be very blessed."

After I got rid of the look of shock on my face I said, "Where do you see this?" And she told me that she saw it over my head. Then she gave me a big hug, reminded me what an amazing God we serve, and walked out. I sat in my office just pondering on what had just been said to me.

A few months later, the lady came back to see me again. She had on the same purple jumpsuit and still no teeth. This time she came in singing a song about Jesus, gave me a big hug, and sat down. The first thing she said to me was, "Isn't God good?" And I said, "Yes, He is!"

That day I was feeling a bit down. I don't remember what was causing me to feel depressed, but I was down that day. I decided to shut the door because I didn't want anyone hearing our conversation. I told her how I was feeling, and I asked her what she saw this time. She looked up to the ceiling and then back down. I asked her again, "Do you see anything?" Feeling very doubtful that she saw anything at all I just stayed quiet.

She looked up to the ceiling again and then back to the floor and she said after a few moments, "He's beautiful."

"Who is beautiful?" I asked.

"Your guardian angel."

I then asked, "Where is he?"

And she said, "Right behind you." I couldn't believe he was right behind me. I wasn't expecting her to say an angel. It was like she handed me a warm blanket. I don't know why, but I thought the angel would be in a corner of my room, not behind me. It was just what I needed that day.

I so wanted to see what he looked like. I asked the Lord to let me see the angel, or at least a piece of his robe. I guess I thought that angels wore robes, at least that's what they wore on TV and in movies a lot of the time. I hesitated before turning around. When I finally turned around, I didn't see anything, but I felt that the angel was behind me. I didn't feel the angel physically, but you know when you feel someone is staring at you and you look up and they are? It was something like that. I know beyond a shadow of a doubt that someone was definitely behind me.

The following weeks I kept looking out for my lady in purple, wishing that she would come. It was so incredible how God was giving her visions for me. That had never happened to me. About another month later, she came again. I was so excited! I gave her a big hug, shut the door, and couldn't wait to for her to tell me what she saw. She sat in my office and right away I asked her if she saw anything. What she said she saw was a little strange. Not as exciting as the other times. She said she saw an egg over my head. She said, "It's not a chicken egg. It's a female egg, and I only see one." I had no idea what all that was about. Then as I was pondering on what she had said she added, "And I don't know why, but I'm hearing December 5th." I had no idea what any of that meant. She then gave me a hug and left.

A couple months went by, and I still hadn't seen her. So, I decided to call her because I wanted to see if she saw any more visions about my life. No one answered. I called several times throughout the week, and no one ever answered. To this day I haven't heard from her or seen her again. I have thought to myself many times that perhaps, just maybe, she was an angel. An angel brought to me at just the right time to send me some more hope for my future baby boy that I was to thank God for, not ask God for, like the Hawaiian pastor told me. Some days it was easy to do, but other days it was so hard to do.

One of my very favorite customers came to my office, a few weeks later, I believe it was to get a copy of her statement. She was the cutest, most stylish, African American woman who always dressed so sharp. She was the pastor of a church not too far from the bank. We always had great conversations about God every time she came to see me. Before she got up to leave, she said she had been praying for me and my husband and our desire to have a baby. The desire to grow our family had been growing and growing in my heart throughout these months. We had had some extended conversations before about how much I desired to be a mom. She then said, "I hesitate to say this because it's kind of strange even to me. While I was praying, I heard December 5th. Does December 5th mean anything to you?" I almost fell out of my chair when I heard her say the words. I then filled her in to why I was so shocked. All she said was, "Well, that's confirmation."

Between the angel with no teeth and the other customer both saying December 5th, my curiosity was peaked. *What in the world is going to happen on that day?* I thought that maybe I would get pregnant, but December 5th came and December 5th went and no baby. I was crushed. How could I have received a word from God from my angel friend and the Hawaiian pastor, and nothing happen? How could He do this to me?

We had been trying to get pregnant for a while and nothing was happening. I'm not going to lie or paint a pretty picture. I was not too happy with God at this time. The toddlers and babies I saw on the street were getting cuter and cuter. I knew so many people were pregnant. At this time, I had like eight friends who were pregnant. This was a very difficult time in my life. I decided to go out with my friends a lot and keep myself entertained.

To top it all off, I decided to buy a convertible. I obviously was not going to have kids anytime soon so I might as well enjoy myself, and enjoy myself I did.

I even took a ten-day trip to Europe to really get my mind off of things.

Has God ever sent someone or something your way to bring you hope? Perhaps you are dealing with something right now that is really hard. God has a way of sending us signs to encourage us, maybe through a song, a sermon, a friend, or a stranger at the grocery store.

My journey was a tough and long one. Sending these people to my work was such an encouragement to me. I know I wasn't alone, but I felt very alone. I wanted a baby so bad. I was walking in a wilderness, a dark, lonely wilderness. But God, sent me hope through these people.

If you are sad, or feel alone, please know that you are not alone. Satan brings on the feeling of loneliness to make us feel so sad and helpless. He wants us to feel invaluable so we will not do great things for God's kingdom.

Ask God to send people to surround you though your wilderness and He will bring you hope and answers. He is a loving God who is always there for you. Reach out to him right now and ask him to fill you with hope and answers. Even when you are in a forest, there is always a sunrise.

Friend, God loves you, and He is always with you even if He is silent.

CHAPTER 7

Heaven Sent Empanadas

No weapon forged against you will prevail, and
you will refute every tongue that accuses you.

ISAIAH 54:17

Acouple years later, I had gone on two more mission trips. One to Peru and one to Nicaragua. We helped out at two orphanages in Peru, and we held a Vacation Bible School in a small town in Nicaragua. Both times in Peru, I kept waiting for an overwhelming feeling to come over me to adopt a child, but it never came. I remembered the instant connection my friend had with that little boy who stole his heart. It took four years, and he was finally able to adopt him and his two siblings.

The prayer the Hawaiian pastor prayed over me that day in my office kept playing in my mind. I kept asking myself, *Did it really happen? Was that prayer really real? Did it really mean anything?* I know that Satan was trying to make me doubt what God had brought to me that day. I was trying so hard to believe that it was real. That God really meant it. It's really hard to hold on to a word God gives you when years keep passing by and you don't have a baby.

My husband and I came to the realization that after so many years of trying to get pregnant we may need to look at another avenue. In 2012, my husband and I decided to see a fertility doctor. We were facing the reality that trying to get pregnant was not going to be easy for us and we were going to need some help. Since that prayer with the pastor in my office, my desire to have a baby was in full bloom. It really was all I thought about. I would see little babies or toddlers and I just wanted to take them home with me. A sweet, adorable little boy would approach me, and I would just melt. I would also tell the mom how blessed she was to have him. Also, at this time, I think everyone and their mother was pregnant. I saw baby bumps everywhere I looked! And at the time I think ten of my friends were pregnant. I would get so discouraged some days. I was invited to a ton of baby showers that year and went to each one, but in the back of my mind I kept saying, *When is it going to be my turn?*

That year I decided it was time to get us both checked out. Someone recommended a fertility doctor nearby, so I decided to go and see him. Everyone in the office was so friendly. I remember being in the room undressing and putting on the hospital gown. You know the one that if you turn around your butt is exposed? I sat there waiting with my husband and wondering what the results were going to be and when the doctor was going to show up in this room.

The doctor finally came in. He did the exam just like an OBGYN does at your checkup. Feet in stirrups. You know the drill. Then he told me to get dressed and to schedule an appointment with the front desk to talk about the results. Let me just tell you, that is not a fun time having to wait a whole week to hear about what could possibly be wrong with you.

The following week we went back to the clinic to hear our results. I was so nervous and wanted to know what was wrong with me. Why can't I get pregnant? We sat there in his office and just waited with anticipation for the doctor to come in. He greeted us very nicely and handed us some papers. He then went into the explanation from all the tests we took. Basically, my egg reserves were low. Then he let me know that there was nothing they could do for my low egg reserve. He also let us know that there were people that got pregnant having a low reserve, but the probability was a lot lower. Then he mentioned about our ages. I was forty-one at the time and my husband was forty-two. He let us know that our age was going to play a big part in all of this, but there were some people our age that have had success.

He gave us many options that we could consider. One was insemination, which is where they take the sperm out of the male and inject it directly into your uterus. They place the sperm closer to the eggs so that they don't have to go far to reach the egg. There were less medications that route. The second was in vitro, or a shorter way to say it is 'IVF.' That is where they take out a few eggs of the female and some sperm from the male. They place them together in a petri dish and see what happens. After a few days, they see how many embryos form. Doing IVF involved many shots that you had to give yourself for about ten days. Then a shot in your butt muscle right before the insemination.

The first one he mentioned sounded so much easier, so we went the easy route. The thought of having to inject myself gave me the heebie jeebies. We made our next appointment to do the insemination. We had to look at my cycle to see when I was ovulating. They gave us the to-do list and off we went.

The insemination procedure was not too bad. It didn't hurt, and there weren't too many medications you had to take. We went in, they did the insemination, and then you were left laying down and they tilted your bed with your feet higher than your head and left you there for a while. Blood was starting to rush to my head, but I was okay. I was excited that we were moving forward in our journey to have a baby. They told me to take it easy the rest of the day and prop my feet up when I could. We were to come back in about a week for the results.

A week went by pretty quick. I went in, they drew my blood, and my husband and I sat in the waiting room until they called our names. Finally, our names were called, and we jumped up. Once again, we sat in the doctor's office and waited for the doctor to come in. My husband and I just sat there in anticipation waiting for the doctor. Why does it feel like an hour when you are waiting for a doctor, when in reality it's like ten minutes? He finally came into the office. We held each other's hands a little tighter. I finally said, "We have been waiting for a week, please tell us our results?" The doctor then handed us some papers and explained what we were looking at. He then let us know that we were still not pregnant.

We were both so disappointed. I cried; my husband held me. Not a fun time for us at all. Then he asked what we wanted to do next. We both were ready to do it again. I wish I could say this route worked for us, but unfortunately this was not the route God had for us to get our baby. We tried it several times and nothing happened. This was a tough time for both of us. I felt like such a failure. I felt like I was broken. It's hard when you want something so bad and your body just can't produce what you want.

We tried insemination all year and in December I finally said, "Okay, I'm ready. Let's do this IVF thing." I wasn't looking forward to all the shots, but I was ready, so, with my eyes closed and with God's help, I was doing this no matter how many shots I had to do. I received a paper with a long list of medications and shots I had to take and inject. *Oh, boy*, I thought to myself. *This is going to be fun.*

That week while I was driving to work, I asked the Lord to give me a theme Bible verse that could carry me through this tough journey. In my spirit, I heard "No weapon formed against me shall prosper." I called my friend right away and shared with her what had just happened. She said, "That is your verse. Repeat when you need it and pray it over yourself when you're taking your medication and giving yourself the shots." And that is exactly what I did. Every time I was about to inject myself or take any medication, I would repeat the words in my Bible verse. I talked to a lot of people who took these same fertility drugs and their reactions to the medication were not good. I can tell you mine were not so bad. The only thing I felt that was different about me was that if I was happy all was good, but if I was sad, it was a downward spiral and very hard to get out. I had to call on my prayer warriors to get me out, and they would pray me out of it. It was like pressing a gas pedal and the pedal got stuck and there was no getting your foot off the pedal. So please, if you are going through this journey make sure you have your prayer warriors.

I didn't have to give myself the shots right away because thankfully God blessed me with a sweet friend who is a nurse practitioner, and she said she would do the shots for me. I just had to go to her house every morning and night to get them done. They had to be done at the same time every day. There were some in the morning and more at night. What a sweet friend to help me out because I was too nervous to give myself my own shots.

One day I was going to a party, and I had to run to my friend's house to get my shots. I was so tired. I just didn't feel like driving all the way to her house which was thirty minutes away. I decided I was just going to try to give myself my own shots. No lie, I closed my eyes and stuck the needle in. I was so nervous, but after I did it, it wasn't too bad. Then I had to do it five more times. I realized that I could do it myself and no longer had to drive to my friend's house to have her do them. It was so nice to just go straight home and relax every day.

In a few days, I was going to have my first IVF done. I had already gone in to have some eggs taken out. They ended up taking five. I freaked out a little. What if I end up with five babies? I was so not ready for that! Then they put the sperm in and waited to see how many embryos formed. After a few days, four embryos formed. I was still a little nervous; not ready to have four babies either.

The night before, I had to get an injection in my butt muscle, which my friend who was the nurse practitioner did for me. Not the best feeling but at least it went quick. The following day I went in for my first invitro. I had so many medications and they had a valium in my list. I had only taken half when they retrieved my eggs. I thought I needed to take the other half. Maybe it was because it was 5:00 a.m. and I wasn't thinking right. I took the other half. Wow, I was holding onto the walls as I walked and had to be walked down the aisle. The nurse asked if I took anything. I then told her I took half a valium. She then informed me that I was only supposed to take it for the retrieval of the eggs. I said, "Whoops, my bad." I was a tad relaxed and didn't feel a thing. It was all a blur since I mistakenly drugged myself up. All I remember them saying is, "We are now inserting your four embryos." And me saying, "I'm not ready for four babies!"

Tricia DeBoer

After they did the procedure, they put you in a cubicle and let you rest. I passed out. It must have been the valium. I woke up to my husband by my chair with a sweet, concerned look on his face. He asked me, "How do you feel?"

I said, "I feel great, honey." Then I asked him, "Are you ready for our four babies?"

He said, "No," and we both laughed. Within thirty minutes we were released to go home and relax. They told me to take it easy the whole week, not to lift anything heavy, and to prop my feel up as much as I could.

There was something so special to know that your body is carrying four embryos. My husband was extra nurturing, waiting on me hand and foot. I felt very pampered. He didn't let me do much. He is such a sweet guy. I was so thankful I didn't have to inject myself every night anymore. I spent that week just lying on the couch and relaxing a lot.

The day finally came when we were going to find out our results. I was so excited to hear how many embryos had made it. I had come to grips that if four came then God would help us handle four. Once again, we were put in his office and had to wait for what seemed like forever.

The doctor finally walked through the door. He sat down and looked at both of us and said, "I'm so sorry. None of the embryos made it." I can't even find the right words to describe how I felt. I was devastated. I cried; my husband held me as I lost it.

These next weeks were very tough weeks. Anything set me off and I would just cry. I was back at work, but very sad. Thankfully I had my husband, family, church family, and co-workers that were there to love on me and hold me when I would just burst out in tears. Two of my friends came over the night I found out that I wasn't pregnant. They brought me cookies and my favorite ice-cream, which is Ben and Jerry's Cherry Garcia. I'm not a drinker, but I got drunk on junk food. For dinner, I had a bag of chips and my favorite ice-cream. I felt so sick afterwards. My friends hugged me and told me they would be there for me if I needed anything. That was a special night. One I will never forget. They tried so hard to make me laugh, and I'll never forget the look of concern on their faces. It was so sweet of them to reach out when I was in my pit of despair. I'm so thankful they came over that night. I really needed them.

A month later I went in to see the doctor and once again he said, "What would you like to do next?" Without hesitation, I said, "I want to do IVF again." So, we started all over. It wasn't my first rodeo. I knew the drill. I knew what to do and what to expect this time, so maybe that's why this time felt easier. Time went by quicker, and I knew to relax more this time. They ended up taking only four eggs out this time around and only three formed into embryos.

This time during the insemination procedure I knew not to take a valium. So, if you took a valium during your insemination by mistake, you are not alone. I was less nervous during the procedure, and I noticed when they injected the embryos in me. They let you see it happen on a T.V. screen. It was very cool. I prayed the whole time up to when I saw them get released into my uterus. I also cheered them on to find the wall and stick to it. Once again, I relaxed when I got home. I prayed so hard that we would finally have our babies. I would enjoy all three of them if the Lord chose to bless us with triplets.

I was working with the youth at our church at the time. One of the leaders shared with us early on that she was pregnant. We talked a lot, and she would always tell me her boobs hurt and that she always felt tired. I was really feeling tired and lethargic those days, too. She asked me if my boobs hurt, and I told her they were unusually sore. Then she said she thought I was pregnant, too. As the days went by, I noticed that certain foods tasted like they were heaven sent. I couldn't get enough of these empanadas at this Cuban place down the street from me. I bought them all the time!

My husband had to go away for work, and I was left alone for a whole week. Just me and my dog, Odi. One day we had no groceries, so I went to the store to buy some. I don't know if I was just hungry, but I almost bought the whole store. I had to lug all the bags in the house by myself, and by the time I finished, I was so exhausted. I ended up falling asleep on the couch that night. The very next day I felt a little different. I had a little more energy and my boobs weren't hurting. I never took a pregnancy test, but I really felt like I was actually pregnant for a few days.

That week I went to the doctor to see how I was doing. Once again, he said, "I'm so sorry. You're not pregnant." I was so sad. Again, I cried, and my husband held me in his arms. The next few days I did a lot of reflecting. I thanked God that He allowed me to feel what it was like to have a baby growing inside of me. I loved that feeling. I was so thankful that the Lord had blessed me with my baby for a few days, and I would cherish those moments always.

LET'S REFLECT

This was a really dark time in my life. I felt like a failure, like I was broken and that there was no way to fix me. Are you going through a difficult, dark time? You're not alone. Those negative thoughts played in my mind daily. I wasn't in God's Word. I was staying far away from my friends.

Then one day, a friend reached out to me and encouraged me. She said that Satan was bringing all that negativity to my mind. She also asked me if I was going to let Satan win. I had two choices: to wallow in my sorrow, or to pick up the pieces and move forward. I chose to move forward. God helped me take each step I needed to take.

I had another friend who ended up in the hospital with her process of fertility, and she encouraged me to enjoy the process. The good, the bad, and the ugly. Because no matter what my story was, it was God's story, and He was writing it for His glory. I hope that encourages you today because it sure encouraged me. No matter what the story is, God is writing it for us to show His glory and grace through it all.

CHAPTER 8

December 5th

For no matter how many promises God has made, they are [all answered] "Yes" in Christ. And so through him the "Amen" is spoken by us to the glory of God.

2 COR. 1:20

A few weeks after the second IVF didn't work, they asked me what I wanted to do next. With no hesitation, I said, "Let's do invitro again!" By now, all of this was getting much easier for me. This time around I was much more positive. I had put it in God's hands and what He ordained to be is what it would be.

I went in for my retrieval and they said they only took three eggs out this time. The time went by much faster this time. My injections were no problem, despite a few bruises they left behind sometimes. I just had a different skip in my step, you could say. Before I knew it, I was going to get my injection in my butt so they could do the insemination the following day. The nurses told me to come in December 6th for the insemination, and I was just excited to see what God was going to bring because I was going to give Him the glory no matter what the result was.

The following day I got a call that my embryos had matured a little faster than normal, so they wanted me to come in for the insemination on December 5th instead. I went into the office feeling great and ready for this insemination to take place. While I was laying on the table, the doctor came in to let me know that there was only one embryo that made it. He asked me if I wanted him to still go ahead with the procedure. I said, "Absolutely!"

Then it all came to me at once. *Wait, today is December 5th, and the angel lady said she heard December 5th, and now I have only one embryo. Does this mean what I think it does? Am I finally going to have a baby?* They went ahead and performed the procedure. I felt great afterwards, and I was ready to go home and take it easy.

When we got in the car, I reminded my husband about the lady and the word she gave me about December 5th. He told me not to get too excited. He didn't want me to be disappointed if it didn't work out. He was helping me keep my emotions in check. I tried to not think about it, but it was always in the back of my mind. *What if this is God's word coming to life?*

Weeks went by and before we knew it, we were going to the doctor to see if I was pregnant or not. We waited patiently for the doctor to come in. The doctor came in and sat down and quickly let us know that the IVF was not successful.

I know you are probably thinking that I broke down and cried, but I didn't this time. Then the doctor asked if I wanted to do IVF again. My husband looked at me and I looked at him, and I said, "Nope, it's time to adopt!"

My husband looked at me and said, "Okay, it's time."

One thing that the Lord put on my heart was when He gives you a word, like the one the lady with no teeth gave me that day, it may not be what you expect, but He always comes through. It will always be in His timing because He always knows best. He told my angel in my office to tell me the words December 5th. I thought I would get pregnant that December, but that wasn't in His plan. The next year I waited again to get pregnant or be pregnant by then, and again that was not His plan. The following year I decided to pursue the fertility doctor route. On that journey, I still did not get pregnant. Then when I was in my last grasp of hope, He had the date change so I would have my insemination done on December 5th. To add to it, only one embryo made it. He was showing me that He is a God of His word. It may not have been the results I thought it was going to be. He spoke it to me and brought it to pass in His own way, on His agenda, not mine. I was really thankful for that. These were times where I felt so much closer to God. If that was His intention, then I am so thankful for how it all worked out for His glory. He was just saying, "Sweet child of mine. I've got this—just trust Me."

The Christmas that came soon after was not the best one for me. I barely decorated our Christmas tree. It was a somber Christmas for us. I really thought that by then we would have a baby to spend Christmas with, but that was not in God's plan for us. Although it was a somber Christmas, I also was in complete peace of what God was bringing by way of His timing. I knew that His plan was perfect, and I just had to trust Him. The first week of January I decided to make an appointment with an adoption agency, and I knew exactly which one I was going to use.

About 15 years ago, I met a friend in one of the daycares I worked at named Carri Uram. She told me one day that she was thinking about starting an adoption agency. I encouraged her to go for it and make it happen. She had two children at the time, had lost her two-month-old, and had adopted a son. She would talk to me about what she envisioned her adoption agency would be like. Her main focus was to have open adoptions. She would explain to me that she wanted the birth mom to still have contact with the adopted parents. Having pictures and some form of contact would make it easier for the birth moms to process giving up their child. If they knew their baby was healthy and doing well, it was easier for them to cope with their loss. She always equated the birth mom giving her child away to almost a passing of a loved one. It was a hard decision for the birth mom to make, but to know the baby was okay made it easier for her to move on.

I loved her heart and motivation behind her desire to start this adoption agency. I knew she was the only person I was going to go through my adoption experience with! Her heart for the Lord and her heart for the birth moms was beautiful to see. That is why I picked her adoption agency called "Special Link." We had our first meeting with her the first week of January because we were ready!

Our first meeting was so amazing! It was such a special time of healing for my husband and me. At our first meeting my friend Carri shared with us about a mom who was trying to get pregnant, she already had two children and had lost her two-month-old son, she decided to adopt a little boy. The little boy was such a blessing and exactly what that family needed. She also shared about the beautiful connection this mom had with the birth mom. Years later this mom ended up going to the doctor for a checkup. After some tests, the doctor let her know that if she had gotten pregnant and had gone full term, she would not be alive today. Her husband would be a widower and would have had to bring up her three children alone. God knew all this ahead of time. He kept her from getting pregnant. This same mom ended up adopting a little girl, and she is happily married with four beautiful children as well as a few grandchildren.

Maybe God kept me from having a baby full term for the same reason. God knows all. I may never know the answer to why I was not able to have a baby on my own. But after I heard that story, I had tears rolling down my face, as they are now. I told God, "Thank you for looking out for me. Thank you for the opportunity to have a baby grow inside of me even if it was for just a few days. Thank you for walking ahead of me and looking out for me and removing obstacles I could not see. You really do love me so much! Thank you that I am still alive!"

Our meeting was so encouraging and just what my husband and I both needed. We were so excited to start our adoption journey. She handed us some profile books of other families that were going through their adoption journey. Profile books consist of pictures of families wanting to adopt. They may have pictures of trips they may have taken and even pictures of nurseries that were decorated and finished. I then thought to myself, *You've got a lot of work to do, missy!* Being that the nursery room we were thinking of using as a nursery was a "dump everything you don't know what to do with" room. I had some work to do!

Carri also gave us an envelope containing things we needed to get done. For example, we had to get our fingerprints, referral letters, and a long essay of why we wanted to adopt. Now, I am quite the procrastinator, so I had no idea how I was going to get all of this done. Well, you know the phrase, "If God leads you to it, He will see you through it"? That was my new motto. He knew that I couldn't get all this done without a village. Because He is such an amazing God, He surrounded me with an incredible village of loving friends.

Remember my friend who gave me my shots during my IVF days? This same friend told me to go to her house and that she would not allow me to leave until all my paperwork was done! And she meant it. I truly believe that if it wasn't for her persistence, I would still be on my adoption journey! And my one friend who has the gift of organizing (I was not given that gift, but I'm so thankful that God put her in my life) came over and helped me clean out my "dump everything you don't know where to put it" room. That was not the easiest job I've ever done, but with her help and lots of laughs, we got it done! Praise the Lord!

A couple of months later I got a call from my friend Carri at the adoption agency. She asked me if I had all of my paperwork ready. I let her know that I was still waiting on a couple things to come in the mail like our marriage certificate that I couldn't find anywhere and our fingerprint results. I asked her why she was asking, and then I said, "Do you have a baby in mind for us?" She said, "I do, but you're not completely ready." After that conversation, I started hustling!

The next time she texted me it was about a birth mom who was having a son. I sent our profile book in to see if she would pick us. That week the strangest thing happened. My husband and I went to Target that night and my husband picked up this onesie that had the Batman symbol on it. Although it was super cute, I just didn't feel like buying it. The birth mom hadn't seen our book yet, and I just didn't feel like buying baby clothes that night. Now the unusual thing was that I normally bought baby clothes all the time! My husband even said, "That is really weird you are not in the baby shopping mood." I then let him know that I felt a little different about buying them that day. I also felt in my spirit that this baby was not going to be ours, and that is exactly what happened. God was not allowing me to be attached to this baby boy.

A few weeks later, I was sent a text about a birth mom with twins. My heart jumped. I was all in! I envisioned the nursery: one side of the nursery baby blue and the other light pink. I was so excited. My husband thought I was crazy. I was praying for the birth mom and the babies growing inside her. The birth mom wanted a couple who did not have any kids. I told my husband, "This is it! These are our babies!" She was still waiting on our profile book, and we were still waiting on one thing to come in the mail to complete all of our paperwork. I was so sure these babies were meant for us. I kept telling my husband, "I don't care if we have to live in a cardboard box. We are getting these kids!" The price for the adoption doubled, and I had it in my mind that I was doing whatever it took to get these babies in my arms!

A couple days later, on a Wednesday, I remember getting a call from my friend from the agency. She told me that the birth mom had not received our profile book and because we were still waiting on one more paper to come in to complete our paper-work, she had to choose the other family who already had two children. Their paperwork was all done, and the birth mom had just found out that she was three centimeters dilated.

My heart sank. I told God that this hurt just as bad as losing my babies. How could He do this to me? I was not happy with God at this time. I kept asking Carri how the babies were, and she kept telling me that she didn't know anything. She then told me something that would resonate in my heart throughout the rest of my adoption journey. She told me, "Sweetie, those babies belonged to this family, not yours. God has a perfect fit just for you. You have to be thankful that God put those babies with the family He chose for those twins." Those words would forever be engraved in my heart. It was a time of healing for me. I had to apologize to God for being mad at Him. I also at this time asked the Lord to let me know beyond a shadow of a doubt that when my baby came, I would just know it.

I sang on a praise team at my church, and there was a song that when I sang it I couldn't hold back the tears. The song goes like this, "He goes before me, He goes behind me, He goes above me, and He goes below me." The tears that came to my eyes every time I sang it was my heart saying, *I know this is so true; it's hard for me to believe it, but I'm so in love with you, Lord, I choose to believe it even when I don't want to.* This song always came to me at the perfect times. When we played it at church or I sang it with my praise team it was always comforting and it was always sent to me at the perfect time, when I needed it most.

A couple weeks later I got a text that there was a birth mom who was having a baby girl. *What? A baby girl?* That had not even been an option until now. It seemed, at the time, all my friends who were pregnant were all having baby boys. I secretly wanted a baby girl, but I was more excited to be a mom more than anything. I would have been happy with any sex as long as I could be a mommy.

We sent in our profile book again and in a few days, we were told that she had narrowed it down to us, and a pastor and his family. My husband said, "You know we have no chance against a pastor." I told him to stop talking negatively. A few days later we were told that the birth mom did pick the pastor. I didn't let myself get too excited because of what my husband had said. I was also guarding my heart because it was so broken over not getting my twins. Then, my friend with the adoption agency shared with me that the pastor had been in the adoption system for three years and had not been matched with a child until this baby girl. He was about to give up and the Lord said, "Now is your time. Here is your baby girl." I was really happy for this pastor. He finally got his answer to prayer. Knowing this back story really helped so much. I was truly happy for this pastor, his family, and their new baby girl.

LET'S REFLECT

Are you going through a season of waiting right now? Are you waiting on God for answers? Can I encourage you that the wait is only God preparing you for your blessing?

The song I shared before was my staple song. I hung onto every word of that song. He goes before you because He is paving a path for you. He knows the bends and turns you're going to be running into, and He tries to redirect us. A lot of times we may not like the redirection, but He's doing it because He loves us and wants the best for us. He goes before us.

Trust Him today. Cry out to Him right now. He's right there waiting for you. He wants us to come to Him and to His loving arms. I pray these words comfort you as it did for me.

CHAPTER 9

This Mama
Needs a Baby

But those who hope in the LORD will renew their
strength. They will soar on wings like eagles; they
will run and not grow weary, they will walk and not
be faint.

ISAIAH 40:31

As I'm writing these words for chapter nine, I have a big smile on face. I hope you feel it. This will forever be my favorite chapter. So, let me not make you wait any longer. A week after we were told that the baby girl went to the pastor and his family, my friend from the agency texted me that she felt that my baby was coming soon. I got chills as I read the words on my phone. A few days later I get a very simple text with these words exactly, "Great situation, baby boy coming in four months, no drugs."

I wish I could say that my heart leaped, but if I'm being honest, it didn't. I think I had my heart set on having a baby girl. I called my husband and he said, "What are you waiting for? Send our profile book!" So, I did. Our profile book made it to the hands of the birth mom with perfect timing. She had five books that were sent her way.

A week later, I got a call from an adoption attorney from Alabama. I really thought this lady had the wrong number. I didn't know anybody from Alabama. She quickly introduced herself and asked if I was sitting down. That was a very strange question. Then she said, "Is your husband there with you?" I said, "You are on speaker, and he is sitting next to me on the couch." Then she proceeded to say, "This is going to feel very surreal, what I am about to tell you." My heart started racing. The next words I heard were, "She picked your book. She picked you and your husband to be the parents of her baby boy!"

I started to cry. I don't have words to describe what I was feeling. I was shocked and in unbelief. My husband hugged me and said, "Is this really happening?" Then something made me ask, "Who else's book did she pick?" Because with all of the other situations we were always up against another family. Then I heard words coming out of her mouth that I couldn't believe. She said, "She only picked your book. She wants no one else." *What?* I was in complete shock! Then the attorney said, "The birth mom loves that you've been married for twenty-two years, and when she saw your picture she said, 'That mama needs a baby!'"

That was the confirmation I needed! I asked the Lord to let me know beyond a shadow of a doubt that this baby was really ours and here it was. She just wanted us! Only us! That's all I needed to go full force and do whatever it took to get that baby in our arms!

At this point we still didn't have the money, but I had heard this phrase by different people in my adoption journey: "If He takes you to it, He will take you through it." I knew that God would make a way. I had such a peace and complete surrender to His plan. I truly believed that somehow, some way, He would make a way. The attorney then said, "The birth mom wants to meet you both. Does next week or the following week work better?" Woah, I so wasn't expecting to meet her so soon. I was pretty shocked how quickly things were going. I felt like I just got on a train, and it was taking off whether I was ready or not! I was ready for this train ride!

Time was going by very quickly. The day we were to meet the birth mom came like a blink of an eye. As I was getting ready in my room to meet the birth mom, I asked my husband if I should put any makeup on. I'm not a big make up person. I put it on occasionally but I'm much more comfortable without it. So, my husband said do whatever makes you most comfortable. Just be you. So, I choose no makeup, just a little chapstick. The funny thing is when we met the birth mom in Alabama, she was also very natural. She had no makeup on either. It gets crazier. Not only could we talk non-stop, but there was a lot we had in common. I love throwing parties. I love to decorate, cook, entertain, and so did she. Right away we decided to follow each other on Pinterest. She also liked to draw and paint just like me. God doesn't play around. We ended our visit with her giving us a copy of her ultrasound and her saying, "I just want to give this baby a better life, and I really feel good with you guys being his parents." Did she just call us parents? The word "parents" just lingered in my thoughts. Let's just say I marinated in it for quite a while. Then my husband said, "Isn't it funny how without the baby being here, he is already so much like the both of us. You are so much like the birth mom, and she is also a quieter person like me." Can I just say one thing? God is in the details!

So many things had to be done before the baby came. I still had to get the money together for the adoption. Can I just interject and say that I would have lived in a cardboard box if we got the twins? It was going to be so expensive! God knew! Getting all this money together was not going to be easy, but I knew that I can do all things through Christ who strengthens me (Philippians 4:13). That had become my new verse.

A month later I had gotten most of the money together for the adoption. My church helped me with some, and my work also gifted a large amount to anyone who adopted, which was a huge blessing. I had already gotten off for my maternity leave because the birth mom was due within a few weeks. I wanted to be completely ready to take off to Alabama as soon as she said the baby was coming.

That year my company had changed the maternity leave from three months to four. I was pretty excited for my four-month break! One day I was walking into a bank to see about getting a little more money that I needed for the adoption. As I was walking in the bank my friend called me and asked me what I was doing. I explained to her I needed just a little bit more money for the adoption, so I was trying to get a loan. She asked me what she could pray for me, and I said, "Pray for favor." And that was it we hung up and I walked in the bank.

When I walked in, there were two people on the teller line. The one teller told me someone would be with me shortly. A few minutes later this gentleman called me to the counter and asked me what I needed. I shared with him a little about my adoption and right away he said I would love to connect you with a friend of mine who also adopted. I said, "Okay." I guess this is something that happens when you adopt. People must like to connect you with other people who have adopted. Then the gentleman said, "You know our church helps out with adoption. Let me call and see what they can do."

Tricia DeBoer

As the gentleman went to the back to call his church, the lady who greeted me walked over to me and had tears in her eyes. I asked her if she was okay and she said, "I was adopted at a young age, and you have moved me with your excitement. That must have been how my mom felt when she was about to adopt me." Now we both had tears. This was again an example of God's perfect timing. At that point, the gentleman had come back and let me know that his church would love to help, but their process takes about a month. I didn't have a month because the baby was going to be born in three weeks if not sooner. It seemed like the gentleman didn't want to take my application at the time. He said he would keep my paperwork and if I still needed the loan to let him know and he would process the loan for me. I thanked him for his efforts and time. He told me that he would pass my number to his friend that also adopted, and that was it. I walked out of the bank.

The following morning, I got a phone call at 8:30 in the morning. I thought it was a little odd because everyone knows I'm off and sleeping in was going to be my new normal until the baby came. I answered the phone and a lady said, "I was given your number by a friend of mine that works for a bank. He told me to call you because you are adopting."

I said, "Oh, hi. Thanks for calling."

She then asked me to share about my adoption journey. So, I shared with her about how things were going and then she shared with me her adoption story. Strangely they were similar in a lot of ways. Then she asked me how much money I needed, and I told her $2,000. Then she asked me how to spell my name. I thought it was a little odd. Then she asked me what I was doing today. I told her I was going to be going to Target that afternoon.

She then said, "Great! I will meet you there."

I then said, "Can I ask why you are meeting me there?"

Then she said, "I have a check for you."

"Wait, what did you say?"

"I will see you at Target this afternoon at one."

With the phone in my hands, I started to sob. I was looking for money at a bank and God wanted to remind me that He is bigger than the bank. God is so amazing! I wasn't expecting any of this! Won't God do it! Let me let you simmer in this for a moment. Especially if you just need a reminder of what a mighty God we serve!

My husband and I had a name in mind for our new baby boy, and it was Jacob. We had picked the name way before we even thought about adopting. Three months before our baby was going to be born, I was hanging out with my girls from my youth group, and we were asking them what their favorite Bible verses were. Four girls had shared their favorite Bible verses, and they all came out of Isaiah. I didn't think much about it.

The following morning my husband said, "I really don't feel like this baby should be called Jacob."

I completely agreed with him and told him I was feeling the same way.

He then asked me, "Did God give you a name?"

I said, "He didn't give me the name but yesterday when I was hanging out with the girls at the coffee shop, four of them shared Bible verses from the book of Isaiah."

My husband said, "Isaiah, huh? What do you think about Isaiah John? He would have my middle name and my dad's first name."

"Wow, Isaiah John DeBoer is such a strong name! It means Salvation of God! I love it!"

Three weeks before Isaiah was born, I was nesting (yes it happens even when you adopt). I had been to Hobby Lobby for the third time that week. I had a bunch of things I was buying in my hand because I figured if I didn't get a shopping cart I wouldn't buy that much. Yeah, that didn't work for me. As I was trying to juggle all these items in my hand, my phone rang. It was the birth mom. She said, "Do you have a minute?"

I said, "Of course. Is everything okay?"

She said, "Yes, I just wanted to run something by you."

"Sure, what is it?" I asked.

She then began to say, "I've been thinking of a name for the baby, and I wanted to see what you thought about it?"

"Absolutely. What name were you thinking of?"

From the other side of the phone came, "Isaiah. What do you think?"

I almost dropped everything I was carrying. I was only able to muster, "I have chills going up and down my legs."

She said, "You don't like it?"

I said, "No, I love it! My husband and I picked that same exact name three months ago!"

She said, "Now I have chills!"

Can I just say that God is in the details! If you ever doubt that then you may need to read this chapter over and over. He not only blessed me financially, but He allowed us to use the name that we fell in love with. The name He gave Isaiah before Isaiah was even an embryo.

A couple weeks later, I was on the phone with the birth mom. She had been having Braxton Hicks a lot. While on the phone she had one of those episodes. I then asked her what it felt like. She described it as a pain with a lot of pressure. The following day we spoke again. I told her that I felt the baby was going to come really soon. I got a text that she was having this pain, but it was more consistent. I called her right away and said, "Go to the hospital right now." I was timing the contractions and they were coming closer and closer together. I finally said, "Okay. Let's get off this phone. Go to the hospital right now, and call me at the hospital when you get a chance." You guessed it. She was in labor. She called me once she got there and talked to me about how everything felt. This was such a special time. I felt like I was going through every step of labor with her. Then she said, "The doctor said they are about to give me Pitocin, so I need to get off the phone. I will call you as soon as the baby comes. I will text you instead since it's three in the morning." A little while later as I was just about to doze off, I got a text. "He's here!! He's healthy, and now I'm going to bed."

The next morning, we took off to Alabama. It was quite surreal driving as a couple with no kids and knowing that on the way back we would be with our son. We arrived at the hospital around two in the afternoon. I was like a crazy woman walking like I was ready to run across the finish line and break the ribbon. We finally found her room, and we walked in. I saw the birth mom laying in the bed and I asked her how she was feeling. She was a little tired but felt good. The next thing she said was, "Do you want to hold him?" as she pointed to the hospital portable crib.

When I looked the direction to where he was, I saw these adorable lips pressed against the plastic, and he was the cutest little bundle wrapped up like a burrito in a hospital blanket. I picked him up gently and brought him to my chest and just held him. The only way I can describe the feeling is that I felt like I was home. A precious moment I will never forget. I just wanted to hold him forever.

Tricia DeBoer

Then I looked at my husband, and he had the sweetest smile on his face. I told him to sit down, and I would place him gently in his arms. My husband just had a beautiful grin on his face, and he was just lit up. At that moment, I realized that this is how Jesus loves His children—just like a mother and father love their newborn son. A love that doesn't know any limits. I get it so much more now.

LET'S REFLECT

You know when I asked if you are in a state of waiting? He was just paving this amazing path to reveal it to you at just the right time.

Please don't get frustrated, or at least don't stay in that frustration. The enemy wants us to get bitter or jealous. The key is to not stay there. Just pass by "it." Don't linger there. Don't let the enemy take a footstool. Don't let the jealousy grow roots or the bitterness to grow branches. One thing really helped me when those feelings would creep in my life. I chose to pray for that person, ask God to bless them more, and celebrate with them in their victories and blessings. Your time is coming.

Remember the Hawaiian pastor who prayed and said, "You will have a son"? That took place in 2006, and September of 2016, ten years later, our beautiful blessing came into our lives. It was so worth the wait. Even though it took ten years, looking back there were so many moments that He was growing me as a mother. I'm so thankful for all God did for me and didn't do. It just wasn't the perfect timing yet.

Thank the Lord for never leaving your side. If you feel like He has I can assure you He never has. God has perfect timing. You will see.

CHAPTER 10

My Vision

In the last days, God says, I will pour out my Spirit on all people. Your sons and daughters will prophesy, your young men will see visions, your old men will dream dreams.

ACTS 2:17

We have come to the last chapter of my book. I want to encourage you and empower you with it. First of all, I want to tell you that you were made with a purpose and for a purpose. There is a God-given destiny for all of us. The question is: Will you go to God and do what it takes to make it become a reality? Here is my journey of finding my purpose, calling, and destiny.

The year before Isaiah came into our lives, I had a vision around three or four o'clock in the morning. In my vision, I saw myself on a stage and I was speaking to young adults. I asked the Lord as I was watching my vision to not show me the whole picture or it was going to freak me out. So instead of showing me the whole room, he only showed me the first couple rows. Then I said, "Lord you have dropped that dream at the wrong house. Go and drop it off two doors down at another house. I can't do this."

Basically, I ignored this vision and didn't tell many people about it and went on with my life. I kept myself busy helping out with my youth group at church. Once we adopted Isaiah, I had many sleepless nights (some of you who don't know what it's like with a newborn, you don't sleep much). During that sleepless time, I had the same vision with a little more detail about two or three times. At that point I told a couple more people, and they said, "Now you can't ignore this. This vision won't leave you." I started thinking maybe this would be a legacy I could leave behind or a ministry Isaiah could continue when I couldn't anymore.

Four months later, I went back to work and reconnected with a friend that I had known a while back. We soon became like sister friends. We encouraged each other daily and sent devotionals throughout the week. This was so encouraging for me and kept me in the Word. One day, Michelle asked me to do the *Daniel Fast* with her. It's a book where every day you read a devotional while you eat a vegetarian diet. You can only drink water, no meat, no sugar, and only veggies and fruit. I actually bought the book a long time ago but never read it. I thought, *Why not? It couldn't hurt.* So, I told her, "Okay, I'm in!"

We sent pictures to each other throughout the day to show that we were eating healthy. That was really helpful because there were so many days I wanted to cheat, then she would send me a pic of how healthy she was eating, and I would feel guilty so I wouldn't cheat. During this time, I would ask the Lord to tell me or show me more of what He wanted me to do. I only saw myself on stage. I didn't know what I was supposed to talk about or anything.

One day at work this customer who I had known for about five years came into my office. She was so happy for me and my adoption and wanted to hear all about it. I couldn't share about my adoption story without talking about all that God had done for me. So, without knowing if she was a Christian or not, I told her everything. I soon found out she was a Christian and she was praising God for everything He did for me through the adoption journey. I decided to share with her about my vision as well. Then I said to her, "You know, I feel like I am supposed to share something from my heart, but I don't have a place to share it. Do you have a youth group?" She then let me know that her church didn't have a youth group at all. I then told her, "Yeah, I'm not feeling led to be a youth pastor." She laughed with me and let me know that I was welcome to use her clubhouse at her apartment complex anytime. I could invite all the youth I wanted, and she could make hotdogs or tacos for them. *Wow, I now have a place*, I thought to myself.

The next week while I talked to God I said, "Lord, now I have a place which is awesome, but I can't have a retreat without music." That week this guy came into my office. I had never seen him before. We talked about how he wrote music, and I shared that I sang on the praise team at my church. I then asked him, "I know this is a strange question, but do you love the youth?"

He said, "I do, but that's a loaded question. Why do you ask?" I then shared about my vision with him, and he asked me, "Do you have a place?" I told him about the clubhouse. You can believe me or not, but I heard *It's bigger than that* in my spirit. Moments later he said, "It's bigger than that." I let him know that I had heard that statement right before he said it. He then said, "That's confirmation, and you are welcome to use my church anytime. If you need music, I'm the music pastor."

What in the world? "Did you say music pastor?" I couldn't believe my ears. *God works fast. I guess God really wants me to do this*, I thought to myself.

That same week, our air conditioning was out at our house, and it was like 80 degrees upstairs. I didn't mind sleeping in the heat as long as I took a shower and went right to bed. My husband was sleeping downstairs where it was cooler, and I was upstairs in the heat. That night I could not sleep. I tossed and turned. I thought, *Maybe He just wanted me to pray.* There were many nights where I couldn't sleep. I would feel like I needed to pray for someone in my prayer language, and I would pray until I would fall asleep. I've been told that this is very common if you are a prayer intercessor.

I realized shortly that He wasn't waking me up to pray. So, I turned the T.V. on and came across a show called "The Camp Meeting." I didn't know why that program would interest me, but I chose to watch it anyway. As I was watching it, on the bottom of the screen I saw #Assignment. Then the man who spoke, Mike Murdock, said, "Today we are going to talk about seven reasons why you should start a ministry." I sat straight up in my bed once I had heard the title. I don't remember all of them, but I do remember a few. The first one was "Whatever makes you angry, whatever makes you cry, that is a clue to your calling. God wants to use you to make a difference in this world." The other one I remember was his fifth point. This one almost made me jump out of bed, pajamas and all, and get in my car and go. It was a surge of adrenaline that went through my body like a lightning bolt. I had never felt that before. He said, "And the fifth reason is that there are so many young people with a calling and no one to lead them." That one really got to me. The Lord was stirring in me this overwhelming desire to help the youth to find their calling and God-given destiny.

And the last one I can remember, I thought to myself, *Well, this one doesn't apply so I'm good.* It was that this thought will

Tricia DeBoer

obsess you and it won't go away. It wasn't obsessing me then, but a few months down the road it was all I could think about. God is funny that way. Something may not apply to your life at that moment, but later on you will remember, and it will completely make sense. That is exactly what happened to me.

The next day, I called the pastor at the church that the music pastor told me about, and he told me that I was more than welcome to use it any day. I chose October 7th because I'm energetic in the fall and my favorite number is seven. The day of the retreat came quite quickly. To be honest, I was so afraid to tell anyone about it. I had no confidence in myself. I had invited my friends and 20 of them came.

When I got to the church, would you believe the music pastor I had met in my office never showed up. His brother was there playing the drums and he told me, "Yeah, my bro tends to flake out sometimes or most of the time." I was so mad! I thought to myself, *How am I supposed to have a retreat without music.* (Side note here, if you have told someone and given your word to do something, please follow through. That was really frustrating because I was really counting on him. Him not showing up shook me up a bit.)

The retreat was going to start at one in the afternoon. My friend who encouraged me to do the "Daniel Fast" came up to me and said, "Your music guy didn't show up. Brush it off. Now, you either start this retreat or call it off. We are here to support you either way. This is your test of obedience. What do you want to do?" Those words woke me back up. The music, or lack thereof, was not going to stop me from moving forward with what God had placed in my heart to do. So, I grabbed the microphone, welcomed everyone, thanked them for coming, and started the retreat.

I had three young adults give their testimony. Then my sweet friend also shared about what God was doing in her life and about the book she had written in seven months. Then she handed me the microphone. When I took the microphone from her hands, the only way I could describe it is to say I was as comfortable as laying on my couch at home. I really thought I was going to be nervous, but once I touched the microphone, I was excited to talk! And talk I did. I was speaking for about 15 minutes when the pastor's wife came in and sat down with a friend of hers. Right after she sat down, I felt something stirring inside me. It felt like an inpouring and filled me up. I ended up talking one hour and thirty minutes without looking at my notes! Can I just encourage you that if you are nervous about speaking in front of people, ask the Holy Spirit to speak through you and you will be surprised what comes out of your mouth!

You have to come empty to God and ask Him to fill you and speak through you. He will fill you, and He will speak through you! You will say things you weren't even planning on saying. That is the Holy Spirit leading and speaking through you. If you are scared of your destiny, it's okay. Remember it's Christ through you that gives you strength. He is the one who puts the desire and passion in you in the first place. Don't take it on as your responsibility. It's Christ through you that will make it happen. Trust Him. You need to say, "Thank you, Lord, for birthing this in me. This is your dream, your purpose, your destiny. Do with it as you please." And get ready because if you give it all to Him, He will blow your mind!

Now let me share what He did for me this year. In March, my friend told me about this retreat that she was going to go to. I really had no money and could not afford it. So, my friend told me one day that they were giving away a free ticket. I told myself,

What are the chances that I would even win it? Well, guess what? I won the free ticket.

This conference catapulted me to my destiny! I felt like a ball that was shot out of a cannon. It was like I was being thrown. I didn't know where or what, but I was being thrown. As I was leaving the conference, I had this overwhelming desire to do a conference just like this one but for young adults. I had been so moved, and I wanted many more people to feel this too. I walked in this conference with not much self-confidence, and I left feeling like God was sending me in this new direction, but I was stronger and more confident. The word I have heard people use to explain this feeling is

"God-fident." I was walking out with God-fidence!

That night I had another vision. It was me speaking to a bunch of young adults and I was in a barn. I only knew one person that had a barn, and I was a little scared to ask this family. One morning as I was driving to work, a friend of mine texted me a YouTube video of Pricilla Shirer. I immediately called the owner of the barn and booked the date. I chose October 5th.

Let me share what moved me about this video. She shared in Luke Chapter 5 about when Simon had fished all night. He had been fishing since the day before, through the midnight hour, and until the morning and caught no fish. I, personally, would have been so frustrated. She said, "Jesus was speaking to a crowd when He saw the fishermen out at sea. He knew they had not caught any fish." In Luke Chapter 5 it also says they were cleaning their nets. They did not put the boat on E-Bay or offer it up on Facebook Marketplace. They were just cleaning their nets for the next day. I'm sure they were just wanting their bed and some sleep. I would have!

Jesus went to Simon and said, "Take me to the deep water. Let's go fishing." I would have said, "Seriously? Out to the same waters that we have been to for hours? Really?"

Jesus would have calmly pointed the way anyway. Then they get to the spot about ten minutes later and Jesus said, "Okay. Cast the net right there." I would have said, "Really? That's exactly the spot we caught nothing, but whatever." Simon cast down his net, and about ten minutes later (this is my version, because I believe Jesus had to build some suspense to prove his point), Jesus said, "Now, pick up the net." I would again begrudgingly say, "Okay, but there's probably not going to be any... whoa! I can't even pick it up!" Then Simon motioned to his other fishermen who were close by. Not a scream, just a wave of the hand, because he was speechless, just like I would have been. The next thing you know, some fishermen came by to help, and Jesus filled their boat, too!

So, what Pricilla points out is that if Simon had had some fish in his boat, Jesus could not have filled his boat. She said you have to come empty to Jesus. That situation you are about to give up on Jesus wants to jump into. What my heart said was that I had been making the retreat about me, putting the stress of it all on me. Jesus just wanted me to come to Him empty. The retreat was His, not mine. I was just to provide the place. He was going to fill it. At that moment of realization, I immediately called the family with the barn. She booked me the barn for October 5th. Won't He do it!

What is He calling you to do? Here are some things I did that motivated me to reach my calling and destiny. *First, I surrounded myself with prayer warriors*, the ones that if you tell them to pray for you because you are down, in minutes they all send you Bible verses, they call you and text you prayers that start with, "Get behind her Satan, you will not block her blessings coming her way!" and you feel better and better throughout the day. Look for friends who will do that for you. Also, be that friend when someone else needs you.

Second, don't have lids in your life. By 'lids' one of my favorite authors, Cindy Trimm (Buy any of her books. She is amazing!), said that if you have a friend who limits you, you have a lid. Get rid of your lids. A lid would be when your friend says, "You're a mom, just be a mom. You don't have time or energy to live out your purpose, girl!" That's a lid. Get rid of the lids in your life. You need friends that say, "God gave you a dream, a calling, a purpose, a destiny. What are you waiting for? Go do it!" Those are the friends God surrounded me with during the writing of this book and the preparation for my second retreat. I would not have accomplished any of it without them.

One of the most important things I try to do every day is *my four-point morning routine.* First is to give God my first seven minutes of my morning. I would say, "Lord, what do you want me to do for You today? Use me as an empty vessel for you." And sometimes I would just be silent to see if He had something for me. Second is to meditate on a scripture, write it down, try to memorize it, share it with a friend, or think of it throughout your day. Third is to listen to worship music and praise Him by singing to Him. The fourth is to make a list of what you want to accomplish that day. When I do all of these things, I have such a productive day. Try and see if it does wonders for you like it does for me.

Another important one is to *say positive affirmations to your-self daily.* I have a sticky note in my planner, in my notebook, and in my devotions that I read every day in my car. This is what my note says, "This is going to be the best week of your life. You're walking in the overflow of God's blessings!" There is something to be said when you speak positively to yourself. Even doctors say when you have a good outlook and are a positive person your outcome of your sickness is going to be a better result. Dr. Emotto did a study on speaking positively. He took a jar of water and only spoke positive things to it. He spoke the words, "love," "peace," "joy," "encouragement," and he also played classical music to it. He had another jar where he only spoke negatively to it. Words like "anger," "hate," and played heavy metal to it. He took a drop of each one and froze the droplet. After it was frozen, he looked at both of them in the microscope. The one he spoke positively to had formed into beautiful snowflakes with different beautiful patterns. The one he spoke negatively to didn't even form a pattern and looked like a deformed, unfinished snow-flake. Our bodies are made of 80% water, so it would make sense that our bodies would respond to what we speak to it. Don't take my word for it. Look it up yourself and try it out yourself.

My positivity helped me get to where I needed to go. When I told myself, *I'm crazy, I can't finish this book, What was I even thinking?* those negative thoughts paralyzed me. When I spoke positively like, *Someone needs to read my words and hear my stories. Even if it touches and helps one person it will all be worth it.* Those positive words and asking for God's help woke me up at 4:00, 5:00, or 6:00 a.m. to work on my book. The Lord woke me up at 5:30 a.m. this morning to finish my book. Being a mom of a two-year-old, a wife, a daughter of an 86-year-old mom with the beginning of dementia, this was no small feat. I had to be intentional, and I also had to give my energy to my family daily. The only time my brain was relaxed enough to write was the morning, and so he woke me up many nights to get this book done for you to read.

And lastly, as Joyce Meyer (Another favorite author. Buy any of her books. They are all great!) said one day in a sermon I was listening to, which became my motto throughout this journey, "Do it afraid!" Do it when your knees are knocking together and when you have sweat going down your back. Do it then. Do it afraid! Because if you wait until you are not afraid, that day may never come. So, do it afraid!

I hope this book encouraged you. If you are reading this book, it was not by accident. I have prayed that the Lord would put this book in the hands of those who needed to know and be reminded that we serve an amazing, mighty, and loving God. So, I leave you with this: Go find your purpose, calling, vision, and God-given destiny! And *do it afraid*!

LET'S REFLECT

Right now, I want you to ask God what His purpose, calling, and God-given destiny is for your life. It took me until I was 48 to find mine. Don't wait that long. The world needs you. A way to find out is to ask yourself what makes you cry or what makes you angry. This is a clue to what change or solution you have to work on to make the world a better place.

Do you want to start a ministry? Do you want to write a book? Do you want to start an orphanage or a clinic in Haiti? The world is your oyster. Your destiny is unique to you. God made you perfectly you.

Embrace who you are and make a difference one person at a time. Be blessed. I pray that you will live out your God-given destiny!

CPSIA information can be obtained
at www.ICGtesting.com
Printed in the USA
LVHW081249240822
726691LV00012B/341